Grandma Loves Me!

This book belongs to:

_____

Grandma Loves Me!

A Keepsake Book of Crafts, Games, Recipes, and Family Records

ABIGAIL R. GEHRING

introduction & select illustrations by MARTHA M. GEHRING

Skyhorse Publishing

This book is dedicated to Nana. I'll never forget sitting in your lap learning to read, pressing flowers we collected together from the meadows, or the stories you shared from your youth and our family's past. Every child should be so blessed as to have a grandmother like you.

And to Grandpa Strat, who was my biggest fan as a five-year-old budding writer. Your energy and determination continue to shape me.

Much of the material in this book originally appeared in the title *Simple Joys of Grandparenting* by the same author.

Copyright © 2015, 2022 by Abigail R. Gehring
Introduction and art on the following pages copyright © 2012, 2022 by Martha M. Gehring: xi, xii, 2, 4, 13, 14, 20, 28, 34, 40, 54, 62, 64, 65, 66, 68, 70, 77, 78, 79, 81, 83, 88, 92, 173, 174–175

Skyhorse Publishing books may be purchased in bulk at special discounts for sales promotion, corporate gifts, fund-raising, or educational purposes. Special editions can also be created to specifications. For details, contact the Special Sales Department, Skyhorse Publishing, 307 West 36th Street, 11th Floor, New York, NY 10018 or info@skyhorsepublishing.com.

Skyhorse® and Skyhorse Publishing® are registered trademarks of Skyhorse Publishing, Inc.®, a Delaware corporation.

Visit our website at www.skyhorsepublishing.com.

10 9 8 7 6 5 4 3 2 1

Library of Congress Cataloging-in-Publication Data is available on file.

Cover design by David Ter-Avanesyan
Cover illustration by Martha M. Gehring

Print ISBN: 978-1-5107-6873-4
ebook ISBN: 978-1-5107-7049-2

Printed in China

Contents

Stories and Nursery Rhymes 97

Introduction

There's a very old tin of metal cookie cutters tucked in the back of my pantry. It comes out a few times a year, mostly around holidays, and when it does I'm transported back to the country home and cookie-making of my childhood. In that home, where anything which "came down through the family" was special, the tin of old cookie cutters was a standout for me! I can see my mother bustling from pantry to table, collecting sprinkles, nuts, dried fruits, at least three kinds of sugar, and—that tin. All the extravagancies to carry out the delightful and important job of making cookie gifts for others (and us!) were assembled, and I couldn't wait to help get the yummy dough rolled out. We had to put on our aprons first, and my red printed one was tied "just so" to make it short enough to keep me from tripping on it, but amply protective, as I'd soon be covered in flour and frosting. As I'd choose a shape, she'd exclaim, "Oh, that one was your great-grandmother Adams'," or, "Grandma Morse gave me these, and this one was handmade by my dear Grandpa Derry." The aroma from the cookies baking, the taste of the dough—how it all comes back! Happy projects and family history lessons from my mother and from my grandparents and beloved Great Aunt Sylvia Derry, too, live to enrich today. Intertwined in those memories is a feeling of safety, comfort, and the anticipation of good things. It is a legacy I yearn to share with our grandchildren!

Several years ago, my first grandson, Atticus, was five years old and I remember how much we enjoyed baking cookies together when he came to visit.

We got out the old cookie cutters—the goose that looks like an upside-down umbrella, the gingerbread man with the pointy cap, the slightly misshapen star. We put on our aprons—the red one for Atticus!—and we were both covered in flour and dough before the oven was even up to temperature. Since then, I've made cookies with four more grandchildren. What a joy to share an activity that had shaped my life in a positive way, and watch the tradition take root in each of their lives.

Often it's the simplest activities that mean the most. Just taking time to listen to what your grandchild has to say can make a big difference in both of your lives. As a young mother, I remember longing for more time to spend with my kids, but so often the days were filled with a busyness that was all-consuming—jobs, errands, housework, meetings, guests. Though life doesn't exactly feel slow even now, certain demands have lessened, and the opportunity to spend undivided hours enjoying time with my grandkids feels like a second chance and an incredible gift. Grandparents offer children the unique opportunity to be the center of attention for a few minutes or an hour or a day. Who else has the time and desire to sit and listen as he shows off every toy in his bedroom? Even the most dedicated Mommy or Daddy is not the best candidate—they've seen every toy already and have a million other things on their minds. Friends are good for a few minutes, but most don't have enough patience for the complete bedroom tour. Grandparents, on the other hand, are in the perfect position to make their grandchildren feel like the most important beings in the world just by being present.

Though no formal activities are needed to create meaningful interaction with children, sometimes playing a game together or sharing a yummy homemade treat can make an already special day with Grandpa or Grandma that much more fun. With this book, you're sure to be prepared next time

you hear those dreaded words, "Grandma, I'm bored." With activities rang-
ing from educational science experiments to creative crafts to silly games,
boredom will have no place in your home. And, for those of you who, like
me, live an airplane trip away from a grandchild, you'll find ideas for long-
distance bonding. There are plenty of kid-friendly recipes in here, too, and
classic nursery rhymes you may have once heard while bouncing on your grandmother's knee. Be sure to flip through the pages at the back, where you'll find
inspiration for sharing family stories with the little ones—they are our future,
and the better they understand us and our history, the longer we'll live on in
their hearts and minds.

I can imagine my grandchildren one day pulling out the old cookie cutters—
probably rusted and even more misshapen than they are now—and placing them
in front of their children or grandchildren. I hope they'll remember our old
farmhouse kitchen with the snow falling outside the windows and the cat curled
up under the stove. I hope they'll remember the stories and laughs and fun we
shared, but through all that, I hope they'll remember how special they are and
how much I love them.

~Martha M. Gehring

"Grandparents are similar to a piece of string—
handy to have around and easily wrapped around
the fingers of their grandchildren."

~Anonymous

Crafts

Berry Ink and Feather Pens

DURING the Civil War, soldiers made ink out of berry juice and used feathers or corn stalks to write letters. Make believe that you and the kids are Civil War heroes and must convey important messages to each other! Or help them use the berry ink and quill pen to write thoughtful notes to teachers, parents, friends, or other relatives. The vinegar helps the ink to retain its color and the salt acts as a natural preservative. Store extra ink in an airtight jar.

You will need:

Strainer

Bowl

Spoon

¼ cup berries (raspberries, strawberries, currants, or any other brightly colored berry will work)

¼ teaspoon vinegar

¼ teaspoon salt

Bird feather

Scissors

Paper

Directions:

1. Put the berries in the strainer, place the strainer over the bowl, and use the back of a spoon to squish the berries so that the juice runs into the bowl. Once all the juice is extracted, discard the berry remains.

2. Add the vinegar and salt to the berry juice. Mix thoroughly.

3. Cut the sharp tip of the feather off at an angle. Dip the quill into the ink and begin writing. Practice on scrap paper until you get the hang of it.

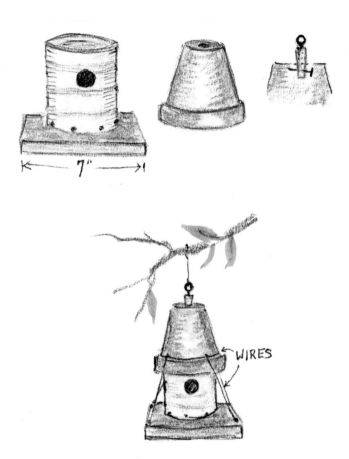

WIRES

Make a Birdhouse!

TEACH kids basic craftsmanship skills with simple, fun projects. This is a small birdhouse that will hang from a tree branch. It's perfect for wrens.

You will need:

Large tin can	Eye screw
Wooden board about seven inches square	Wire
Carpet or upholstery tacks	Small nails
Earthen flowerpot	Waterproof tape
Small cork to plug up the flowerpot hole	

Directions:

1. Mark the doorway on the side of the can and cut the opening with a can opener. Cover the sharp edges of the opening with waterproof tape.

2. Fasten the can to the square board by driving large carpet tacks through the bottom of the can and into the board.

3. Invert the flowerpot to make the roof. Plug up the drain hole to make the house waterproof (use a cork or other means of stopping up the hole).

Continued on next page . . .

4. Screw the eye screw into the top of the plug to attach the suspending wire. Drill a small hole through the lower end of the plug so that a short nail can be pushed through after the plug has been inserted to keep it from coming out.

5. Fasten the flowerpot over the can with wire, passing the loop of wire entirely around the pot and then running short wires from this wire down to small nails driven into the four corners of the base.

6. Now the birdhouse can be painted and hung on a tree.

"A child needs a grandparent, anybody's grandparent, to grow a little more securely into an unfamiliar world."

~Charles and Ann Morse

Coupon Book

HELP the grandkids make a personalized coupon book for their mom or dad. If you want, add a few "bonus" babysitting coupons from Grandma!

You will need:

> Construction paper or computer paper
> Scissors
> Markers, crayons, stickers, or other decorations
> Hole punch and yarn, or stapler
> Small piece of cardboard or heavier card stock

Directions:

1. First, work together to make a list of things the parent will appreciate, such as:

Setting the table	Breakfast in bed
A hug	Thirty minutes of quiet time
Sweeping the floor	An impromptu song or joke

2. Once you have a good long list, cut a piece of construction paper or computer paper into eight rectangles. To make it easy, fold the paper in half lengthwise, unfold, and cut along the crease. Stack the sheets, fold widthwise, unfold, and cut along the crease. Stack all the sheets, fold widthwise, unfold, and cut along the crease one last time.

3. The kids can write what each coupon is for and then decorate with markers, stickers, sparkles, etc. Create a front and back cover out of the cardboard or card stock and decorate.

4. Punch a hole in one corner of the coupon book and tie with yarn, or staple the pages and cover along one edge.

Finger Paint

WHY buy finger paints when you can make your own in a jiffy? For this recipe you can use food coloring that comes in a little bottle or go natural and tint the paint with beet juice for red, blueberry juice for blue, and carrot juice for yellow.

You will need:

¹⁄₃ cup cornstarch	2 cups cold water
3 tablespoons sugar	Food coloring

Directions:

1. Mix cornstarch, sugar, and water in a 1 quarter saucepan.

2. Cook and stir over medium heat about five minutes or until thickened. Remove from heat.

3. Divide the mixture into separate cups or containers. Tint mixture in each container with a different color. Stir several times until cool. Store in airtight containers. Works best if you use the paint the same day you make it.

"Just when I thought I was too old to fall in love again, I became a grandparent."

~Unknown

Handmade Valentines

VALENTINES can be as simple or elaborate as time and creativity allow.

Here are several ideas for different types of valentines:

- Paste a doily onto a piece of colored construction paper and cut it into a heart shape.

- Cut out two paper hearts in different colored paper, making one slightly bigger than the other. Paste the smaller one on top, so that the larger heart forms a border all the way around the inner heart. Decorate the edge of the inner heart by pasting lace around the edge or drawing a pretty border. Write a message in the center.

- Use wrapping paper, stickers, wallpaper samples, or magazine clippings to add texture and variety.

- Make a heart butterfly card. Paste two hearts together tip to tip to form the wings of a butterfly. Use pipe cleaners for the body and feelers.

- Paste several hearts together tip to tip to form a flower. Paste a small circle of paper in the center where all the "petals" join.

Make a Sundial

SUNDIALS have been used for well over 5,000 years as a means of telling time based on the sun's position. The vertical axis, or gnomon (in this case a chopstick), casts a shadow over the horizontal axis (the wooden disk). The shadow moves as the sun travels across the sky. You can tell what time it is by seeing where the shadow falls.

You will need:

Wooden disk or rectangle
Chopstick or wooden dowel
Drill
Air-dry clay

Paint
Permanent marker
Spray acrylic sealer

Directions:

1. Drill a hole in the wood. The hole should be just large enough for the wider end of the chopstick to fit.

2. Let your grandchild press the clay into the hole and stick the wide end of the chopstick firmly into the clay. Be sure the chopstick is completely vertical—not leaning one way or the other. Allow the clay to harden. If desired, paint the disk and gnomon (chopstick).

3. Place the sundial in a sunny spot outdoors early in the day. Every hour, on the hour, make a mark where the gnomon's shadow falls and place a number near the mark to indicate the time. You may want to do this in pencil first and then outline it with permanent marker. When all twelve hours are marked, spray the entire sundial with a clear acrylic sealer. Allow to dry and then apply a second coat.

"The laughter of a child is the light of a house."
~African proverb

Make Paper

INSTEAD of throwing away your old newspapers, office paper, or wrapping paper, recycle it to make your own unique paper! The paper will be much thicker and rougher than regular paper, but it makes great stationery, gift cards, and giftwrap.

You will need:

Newspaper (without any color pictures or ads if possible), scrap paper, or wrapping paper (non-shiny paper is preferable)

2 cups hot water for every ½ cup shredded paper

2 teaspoons instant starch (optional)

Blender or eggbeater

Mixing bowl

Flat dish or pan (a 9 x 13-inch or larger pan will do nicely)

Rolling pin

8 x 12-inch piece of non-rust screen

Four pieces of cloth or felt to use as blotting paper, or at least one sheet of Formica

10 pieces of newspaper for blotting

Directions:

1. Tear the newspaper, scrap paper, or wrapping paper into small scraps. Add hot water to the scraps in a blender or large mixing bowl.

2. Beat the paper and water in a blender or with an egg beater in a large bowl. If you want, mix in the instant starch (this will make the paper ready for ink). The paper pulp should be the consistency of a creamy soup when it is complete.

3. Pour the pulp into the flat pan or dish. Slide the screen into the bottom of the pan. Move the screen around in the pulp until it is evenly covered.

4. Carefully lift the screen out of the pan. Hold it level and let the excess water drip out of the pulp for a minute or two.

5. With the pulp side up, put the screen on a blotter (felt) that is situated on top of some newspaper. Put another blotter on the top of the pulp and put more newspaper on top of that.

6. Using the rolling pin, gently roll the pin over the blotters to squeeze out the excess water. If you find that the newspaper on the top and bottom is becoming completely saturated, carefully add more and keep rolling.

7. Remove the top level of newspaper. Gently flip the blotter and the screen over. Very carefully, pull the screen off of the paper. Leave the paper to dry on the blotter for at least twelve to twenty-four hours. Once dry, peel the paper off the blotter.

Add variety to your homemade paper:
· To make colored paper, add a little bit of food coloring or natural dye to the pulp while you are mixing it in the blender or with the egg beater.

- You can also try adding dried flowers (the smoother and flatter, the better) and leaves or glitter to the pulp.

- To make unique bookmarks, add some small seeds to your pulp (hardy plant seeds are ideal), make the paper as directed, and then dry your paper quickly using a hairdryer. When the paper is completely dry, cut out bookmark shapes and give to your friends and family. After they are finished using the bookmarks, they can plant them and watch the seeds sprout.

Pinecone Birds

PINECONES lend themselves to all sorts of fanciful creations. With a little string, some construction paper, and a marker you can transform pinecones of varying shapes and sizes into a flock of birds!

You will need:

Pinecones (any size or shape)

Pencil

Scissors

Construction paper

Glue

Colored marker

Strong thread or dental floss

Directions:

1. The pinecones will be the bodies of the birds. To add feathers, cut out leaf-shaped pieces of construction paper, draw vein patterns on the pieces, and glue them to the sides or one end of the cone.

2. For a turkey, tilt a round pinecone on its side and glue the feathers upright to the top petals of the cone. Add a neck and head with more construction paper, drawing on the eyes. For an owl, a round cone can be stood upright on its bottom petals—just add big round eyes and an oval beak cut out of construction paper and you have a wise old owl! For a blue bird, use an elongated cone and glue the construction paper wings to either side. Glue a head to the bottom petals of the cone. Don't forget to draw the beak and eyes!

3. To hang your bird ornaments, secure the strong thread or dental floss around a pine cone petal and tie in a knot. Hang them on your Christmas tree or in the window!

"What a bargain grandchildren are! I give them my loose change, and they give me a million dollars worth of pleasure."

~Gene Perret

Potato Prints

HERE'S a project that is great for any age—prints can be very sophisticated or very simple and can be used to decorate stationery, tee-shirts, wrapping paper, or placemats. You may even want to print a few tea towels or cloth napkins for yourself!

You will need:

2 or 3 potatoes	Paring knife
Paper or fabric	Acrylic or fabric paint
Small metal cookie cutters	Paintbrush or sponge

Directions:

1. Slice the potatoes in half and press a cookie cutter into the flesh of one half. Use the knife to trim away the flesh from around the cookie cutter so that the shape sticks up about ¼ inch.

2. Remove the cookie cutter and use the paintbrush or sponge to paint the protruding shape.

3. Use the potato like a stamp. Have the kids experiment on scrap paper until they get a feel for how much paint to use.

Pressed Flowers and Leaves

PRESSED flowers can be used to decorate stationery, handmade boxes, bookmarks, scrapbooks, or picture frames. Kids can glue pressed wildflowers to a blank book and add species names and descriptions to make their own field guides.

You will need:

Large book or newspapers	Weights
Blotting paper	Leaves, ferns, or flowers

Directions:

1. Have a large book or a quantity of old newspapers and blotting paper, and several weights ready.

2. Use the newspapers for leaves and ferns. Blotting paper is best for the flowers. Both the flowers and leaves should be fresh and without moisture. Place them as nearly as possible in their natural positions in the book or papers, and press, allowing several thicknesses of paper between each layer.

3. Remove the flowers and leaves onto dry papers each day until they are perfectly dried. Some flowers, like orchids, must be immersed—all but the flower head—in boiling water for a few minutes before pressing, to prevent them from turning black. In order to preserve your flowers forever, get a blank book or pieces of stiff, white paper on which to mount your preserved flowers and leaves. You can glue them down to the paper

with hot glue or regular Elmer's glue. The sooner you mount the specimens, the better. Place them carefully on the paper and, beneath each flower or leaf, write the name of the plant, where it was found, and the date.

Collages

COLLAGES are a great way to let kids unleash their creativity—and to make use of all those old magazines you have lying around.

You will need:

Magazines and catalogs	Paper or poster board
Scissors	Paste or rubber cement

Directions:

1. Kids can choose a theme (flowers, animals, my favorite things, places I'd like to go, etc.) or just find images or words that inspire them as they flip through the colorful magazines.

2. After cutting out the pieces they'd like to include in the collage, they can paste them onto the paper or poster board in any way they like.

3. You might help them outline their name or a word in big block letters, which they can then fill in with the images. For example, you could write the word "JOY" for them to fill in with pictures of happy people or fun things.

Sand Jars

IF you're looking for a simple project that will have the kids happily occupied for at least a good hour, sand jars are perfect. With minimum preparation and very little cleanup, you might enjoy making sand jars as much as the little ones!

You will need:

Sand or salt

Paper cups

Food coloring

Glass jars

Toothpicks

Directions:

1. Fill several paper cups half full with the sand or salt. Add a few drops of liquid food coloring in each cup and mix with a spoon until the color is evenly distributed.

2. Kids can begin to layer the colored sand or salt in the jar, alternating colors. Tilt the jar back and forth as layers are added or stick a toothpick in the layers to create interesting patterns.

Sock Puppets

FINALLY, a good use for all those socks that have mysteriously lost their mates! Size and color don't matter—any sock will make a fabulous puppet with a little creativity. Once you're done, put on a puppet show.

You will need:

Socks

Fabric glue

Permanent marker

Buttons, cotton balls, yarn, scraps of fabric, or other decorations

Directions:

1. Help the kids create imaginative puppets by decorating the socks as characters. Glued-on buttons make great eyes, yarn or cotton balls make great hair and beards, and mouths can easily be drawn with a permanent marker.

2. Use scraps of fabric to make clothes for the puppets. You can even add beaded necklaces and earrings, sunglasses, or hats. Or turn the puppets into animals by sewing on floppy fabric ears or drawing whiskers.

Terrariums

TERRARIUMS are miniature ecosystems that you can create and keep indoors. Terrariums can contain only plants or can be homes for lizards, turtles, or other small animals. If you opt for a pet, be sure your grandkid is capable of taking care of it, or be prepared to do so yourself.

The size of the terrarium can be as large as a fish tank or as small as a thimble. Bowls, teapots, jars, and bottles have all been successfully transformed into miniature indoor gardens. Terrariums can be fully enclosed or can have an open top to allow fresh air to circulate. Because one of the benefits of a terrarium is the oxygen that the plants contribute to the air, these directions are for an open top terrarium.

You will need:

Container (preferably a clear glass container, so you can easily see your miniature garden)

Coarse sand or pebbles

Sphagnum moss

Soil

Seeds or seedlings

Water

Ornaments (optional)

Directions:

1. Place a half-inch to one-inch layer of coarse sand or pebbles in the bottom of your container. This will help the soil to drain properly.

2. Add a layer of moss over the pebbles. The moss acts as a filter, allowing the soil to drain but not to seep down into the pebbles.

3. Pour the soil over the moss and spread evenly. How much soil you use will depend on how big your container is and how large the plants will grow. Pat the dirt down firmly.

4. Plant the seeds or seedlings. Think carefully about how you want the plants to be arranged. You may want taller plants in the center and shorter ones toward the outside so that you can see them all. Add pretty stones, pinecones, figurines, or other ornaments, if desired.

5. Place your terrarium in a sunny spot and water it regularly.

Edible Playdough

EASY to make and easy to clean up, playdough can turn any boring rainy afternoon into hours of fun and creativity. With this recipe, the kids can even eat the fruits of their labor! By the way, if one of your little munchkins happens to be on a gluten-free diet, this recipe is entirely safe (just be sure the powdered sugar uses corn starch rather than wheat starch—most brands do, but it's worth double-checking).

Once the dough is made, the possibilities are endless. Kids can roll it out and cut it in shapes with cookie cutters, shape it into cakes and cookies and pretend they're running a bakery, mold it into monsters, snakes, or pinch pots . . . or anything else their imaginations fancy!

You will need:

1 cup creamy peanut butter   2 cups powdered sugar
$1/3$ cup honey   1 teaspoon vanilla (optional)

Directions:

1. Combine all ingredients in a bowl, mix thoroughly, and start sculpting (and snacking)!

2. Store in an airtight plastic baggie.

"Between the earth and sky above, nothing can match a grandparent's love."

~Unknown

Games
and Activities

"Grandchildren don't stay young forever, which is good because grandfathers have only so many horsey rides in them."

~Gene Perret

Bob for Apples

THIS old-fashioned game is traditional for Halloween or harvest parties, but is lots of fun for any gathering!

You will need:

Apples
Large basin
Water

Directions:

1. Fill a large basin with water and place several apples in it. The goal is to catch an apple with your teeth—without using your hands. The first person to bite into an apple wins.

2. For a more challenging game, the winner must eat the whole apple. Anyone who plays is likely to get their face and shirt wet, so be prepared with a towel and perhaps some dry clothes for after the fun is over.

Plant Magic

DID you ever wonder how water gets from a plant's roots to its leaves? The name for this is "capillary action." If you're lucky enough to have a whole day with the grandkids, this is a fun and fascinating way to learn a bit more about how plants "drink" water. Set an alarm clock so you remember to check in on your results every two hours.

You will need:

- 4 same-size stalks of fresh celery with leaves
- 4 cups or glasses
- Red and blue food coloring
- Measuring cup
- 4 paper towels
- Vegetable peeler
- Ruler
- Old newspapers

Directions:

1. Lay the four pieces of celery in a row on a cutting board or counter so that the place where the stalks and the leaves meet matches up.

2. Cut all four stalks of celery four inches (about ten centimeters) below where the stalks and leaves meet.

3. Put the four stalks in four separate cups of purple water (use ten drops of red and ten drops of blue food coloring for each half cup of water).

4. Label four paper towels in the following way: "two hours," "four hours," "six hours," and "eight hours." (You may need newspapers under the towels.)

5. Every two hours from the time you put the celery into the cups, remove one of the stalks and put it onto the correct towel. (Notice how long it takes for the leaves to start to change.)

6. Each time you remove a stalk from the water, carefully peel the rounded part with a vegetable peeler to see how far up the stalk the purple water has traveled.

7. What do you observe? Notice how fast the water climbs the celery. Does this change as time goes by? In what way?

8. Measure the distance the water has traveled and record this amount.

9. Make a list of other objects around your house or in nature that enable liquids to climb by capillary action. Look for paper towels, sponges, old sweat socks, brown paper bags, and flowers. What other items can you find? Capillary action happens when water molecules are more attracted to the surface they travel along than to each other. In paper towels, the molecules move along tiny fibers. In plants, they move through narrow tubes that are actually called capillaries. Plants couldn't survive without capillaries because they use the water to make their food.

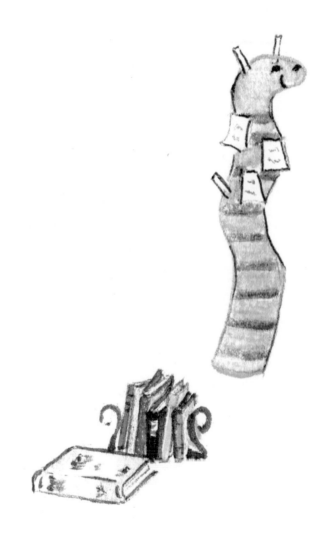

Bookworm

GET the kids excited about reading with this fun bookworm that will keep track of how many books they've read. If your grandchild visits often, hang it on a wall in your home. If not, send it home with the child and ask about their progress when you speak on the phone.

You will need:

    Three-foot-long strip of felt, construction paper, or poster board
    Scissors
    Markers
    Index cards

Directions:

1. Cut out the felt or paper in the shape of a long, curvy worm. Make it at least three inches wide and about three feet long. Cut a circle for a head and glue it to the worm's body. Draw evenly spaced horizontal lines across the worm's body and two eyes and a smile on the head.

2. Hang the bookworm on the wall in a fun spot. Whenever your grandchild finishes reading a book, he or she can write the name of the book and the date on an index card. They can even give the book a rating—one star means it was terrible, five stars means it was excellent. Ask them to explain why they do or don't like each book.

3. Tape or tack the index cards to the worm's body. Once the body is full of cards, have a little celebration—maybe a trip to the local bookstore or a special treat!

"A grandfather is someone with silver in his hair
and gold in his heart."

~Author Unknown

Car Games

LONG car rides don't have to lead to whining, arguing, or desperate boredom. As soon as the going gets tough, start an interactive game—play one of these or make up your own. You'll be amazed how quickly the miles fly by.

Twenty Questions

One person chooses a specific person, place, or thing and then only reveals to the other players what the category is. The others can ask up to twenty "yes" or "no" questions in an attempt to figure out what the person has in mind. Whoever guesses correctly first wins.

I Spy

One person chooses an object in the car and tells the other players what letter it starts with: "I spy with my little eye, something starting with the letter D." The other players look around and try to guess what the object is.

License Plate Alphabet

Look for each letter of the alphabet on license plates of surrounding cars. See how fast you can get to Z. If cars are few and far between, you can search for letters on signs or on objects in the car, too.

Continued on next page . . .

License Plate Bingo

Copy a map of the United States to bring on our road trip. Every time you see a license plate from a new state, check it off on the map. When you have all the states checked off, bingo! For shorter road trips, limit the game to a your region (such as New England states).

Rhyme Time

One person says a word and the others take turns saying a word that rhymes. If they take too long or repeat a word that someone has already said, they're out until the next round. The last person left rhyming wins!

Long-Distance Activities

IF your grandchild lives a long way from you, there are still ways to build a closer relationship. Here are some ideas to get you started.

- Make letter-writing fun for your grandkids. Buy blank postcards from a stationery store, write your address on them, and add a stamp. Kids can draw or write on a card and then send it to you in the mail!

- Buy two scrapbooks and send one to your grandchild, keeping one for yourself. Take turns sending each other special things that remind you of the other—postcards, pictures, newspaper or magazine clippings, fun stickers, etc. Place the items in your scrapbook and label them with the date. When you visit each other, look through the other's scrapbook and reminisce about why you sent each item.

- Email and text messaging make keeping in touch easier than it ever was before, especially with slightly older children. Stay in touch every day with simple games such as "Alphatext." For this game, text each other how you're feeling every day using at least one word that starts with the letter of the day. For example, on day one, you could text, "Amazing!" Day two might be "Bored," etc. This is also a great, low-pressure way to spark conversations.

- Write a book together. Buy a journal or notebook and write the first page of a story and then send it to your grandchild, who will write the next page and send it back. Older children may prefer doing this via email. For younger children, you can do the writing and they can do the illustrations.

"If becoming a grandmother was only a matter of choice, I should advise every one of you straight away to become one. There is no fun for old people like it!"

~Hannah Whithall Smith

Compost Lasagna

TEACH the kids about composting with this fun and easy project. You'll get to watch your produce scraps decompose and see how some materials don't.

You will need:

- 1 (2-liter) clear plastic bottle
- 2 cups fruit and vegetable scraps
- 1 cup grass clippings and leaves
- 2 cups soil
- Newspaper clippings or shredded paper
- Styrofoam packing peanuts
- Magic marker

Directions:

1. Layer all your ingredients, just like you'd make a lasagna. Start with a couple inches of soil, then add the produce scraps, then more dirt, then the grass clippings and leaves, more dirt, the Styrofoam, more dirt, the shredded paper, and top it all off with a little more dirt.

2. Use the magic marker to mark the top of the top layer. Then place the bottle upright in a windowsill or another sunny spot. If there's a lot of condensation in the bottle, open the top to let it air out.

3. Once a week for four weeks check on the bottle and notice how the level of the dirt has changed. Mark it with the marker.

4. At the end of four weeks, dump the bottle out in a garden spot that hasn't been planted, or add it to your compost pile. Notice which items decomposed the most. Remove the items that didn't decompose and discard them in the trash.

Garden Party

A party in the garden is a great way to celebrate a birthday, last day of school, or other special event. And it will show kids how much fun gardens can be. For invitations, cut large flower shapes out of construction paper and let the kids paste pictures from seed catalogs or gardening magazines onto one side. On the other side, write the date, time, and place of your party.

The garden itself will serve as a beautiful backdrop for your celebration, but if you want to go further, choose seasonal decorations such as bouquets of lilacs and apple blossoms in spring, daisy chains in summer, and pumpkins and cornstalks in fall. Once at the party, kids will enjoy decorating their own clay flowerpots by painting them with acrylic paints or, for older kids, by using a glue gun to attach stones or beads to the outsides of the pots. Then provide seeds and soil so they can bring a potted plant home and watch it grow.

Have a contest to see who can make the most creative faces or sculptures out of fresh produce—and then eat the fun creations! Scavenger hunts are always a hit. Provide a chart showing different types of leaves, grasses, and flowers and see who can find all the items and check them off the chart first. Kids will enjoy coming up with their own games, too. Just spending time together in the garden will create lasting fun memories.

Papier-Mâché Piñata

THIS project can get a little messy, but is well worth it. The only thing better than having a piñata at a party is having a piñata you made yourself!

You will need:

Large balloon

Newspaper

1 cup flour

1 cup water

Crepe or tissue paper in various colors

Directions:

1. Cover your table or floor with newspaper.

2. Mix the flour and water together in a large bowl to create a thick paste. Tear several newspapers into strips that are one inch wide and six to eight inches long.

3. Blow up the balloon as large as possible and tie it closed.

4. Soak the newspaper strips in your paste and cover the balloon with them, leaving a space at the top large enough that you can pour the candy in later. You want the newspaper strips to be well covered with paste, but not dripping, so remove excess paste with your fingers before sticking them to the balloon.

5. Allow the balloon to dry and then repeat with two more layers of paste-covered newspaper strips.

6. When the final layer is dry, stick a needle in the opening to pop the balloon.

7. To decorate the balloon, tear two-inch-long strips of colored tissue paper. Cover the piñata with a thin layer of paste and, starting at the bottom of the balloon, paste one ring of strips all the way around the balloon, leaving the bottom ends of the strips hanging loose. Start the next circle of paper slightly higher on the balloon, so that it partially overlaps the first circle. Continue up to the top of the balloon.

8. Fill the piñata about one-third full with candy. Poke four holes around the top and thread strings through to hang the piñata for the party.

"Grandma always made you feel she had been waiting to see just you all day and now the day was complete."

~Marcy DeMaree

How Soap Works

TEACH kids how soap cleans with this simple experiment.

You will need:

2 Mason jars   Oil

Water   Liquid soap

Food coloring

Directions:

1. Half-fill two Mason jars with water and add a few drops of food coloring. Pour several tablespoons of oil into each jar (corn oil, olive oil, or whatever you have on hand will be fine). You will see that the oil and water form separate layers. This is because the molecules in oil are hydrophobic, meaning that they repel water.

2. Add a few drops of liquid soap to one of the jars. Close both jars securely and shake for about thirty seconds. The oil and water should be thoroughly mixed.

3. Let both jars rest undisturbed. The jar with the soap in it will stay mixed, whereas the jar without the soap will separate back into two distinct layers.

   Why? Soap is made up of long molecules, each with a hydrophobic end and a hydrophilic (water-loving) end. The water bonds with the hydrophilic end and the oil bonds with the hydrophobic end. The soap serves as a glue that sticks the oil and water together. When you rinse off the soap, it sticks to the water, and the oil sticks to the soap, pulling all the oil down the drain.

Have a Tea Party

RATHER than your usual snack time, prepare a special tea party. Set a small table with a nice tablecloth and a china tea set, if you have one (and won't be devastated if something breaks—accidents happen). If not, mugs and small plates are just fine! Doilies and fresh flowers will make the table especially festive. Teddy bears and dolls make welcome additions to the guest list.

Once the table is ready, heat a kettle of water and bring out the dainty treats. Serve sandwiches cut in fun shapes with cookie cutters, miniature cupcakes, or biscuits and jam.

To make Cambric tea, heat milk and fill each teacup half full. Add the hot water to fill the cups and sweeten with honey. Candy canes make delicious straws—break off the curvy top and use the candy cane to stir the tea in the cup. As the candy cane begins to melt, a hole will form in the middle, through which you can drink the tea (once it has cooled off suitably).

Be sure to teach the little ones proper manners for tea time, but keep it fun and lighthearted!

Build an Indoor Fort

IS it rainy or too hot or cold to play outside? Build an indoor fort! You can make it very simple or be very creative in your engineering techniques. With these tips the grandkids will be amazed by your fort-making skills.

- Drape a blanket or sheet over a table or two chairs so that the edges come to the ground, creating a tent.

- To make a tent the little ones can stand up in, secure corners of a sheet to tall furniture, bedposts, or the top of a door. If the middle of the sheet is sagging, use a broom handle or chair to prop it up.

- Stretch a blanket over the gap between two twin beds.

- Prop up cushions or pillows near sturdy furniture to make walls and use a blanket for the roof.

- Turn a large cardboard box upside down and cut windows and a door in it. Use magic markers to draw curtains, shutters, etc.

- Create an entrance to the fort by tilting cushions together to form a tunnel.

- Cover the floor of the fort with soft blankets and quilts.

- String Christmas lights around the fort to make it extra festive.

- After the hard work is done, cozy up inside and read a story together by flash-light.

"We should all have one person who knows how to bless us despite the evidence. Grandmother was that person to me."

~Phyllis Theroux

Plant Art

ARE the grandkids coming to visit for a whole week in the summer? Take advantage of the opportunity to teach them about photosynthesis with this neat experiment. See what happens when a plant (or part of a plant) doesn't get any light!

You will need:

Paper   Plant with large leaves
Scissors

Directions:

1. Cut three paper shapes about two inches by two inches. Circles and triangles work well, but you can experiment with other shapes, too. Clip them to the leaves of a plant, preferably one with large leaves. Either an indoor or an outdoor plant will do. Be very careful not to damage the plant.

2. Leave one paper cutout on for one day, a second on for two days, and a third on for a week. How long does it take for the plant to react? How long does it take for the plant to return to normal?

Photosynthesis means to "put together using light." Plants use sunlight to turn carbon dioxide and water into food. Plants need all of these to remain healthy. When the plant gets enough of these things, it produces a simple sugar, which it uses immediately or stores in a converted form of starch. We don't know exactly how this happens, but we do know that chlorophyll, the green substance in plants, helps it to occur.

Scavenger Hunt

SCAVENGER hunts are particularly fun at parties or when there are several kids to participate, but a child can play alone, too. They can be played indoors or outdoors and are easy to put together last minute.

Make a list of items the kids will hunt for. When it's time to start, give the kids the list and see how quickly they can check off (or bring back) each item. Here are some ideas, though, of course, you should choose things that can be found in your area:

Outdoor Scavenger Hunt

Leaf	Spider
Something blue	Bird
Something smooth	Nut
Something prickly	Seashell
Moss	Flower
Pinecone	Vegetable
Something that moves	Animal track
Feather	Seed
Ant	

Continued on next page . . .

Indoor Scavenger Hunt

Hat
Hairbrush
Pencil
Something silly
Keys
Something cold
Something bumpy
Spoon
Toy

Something that makes noise
Towel
Book
Penny
Magazine
Ruler
Something pretty
Something that smells good

"Your children are your rainbows and your grandchildren are your pot of gold."

~Author Unknown

Story Time

THIS game can be played anytime, anywhere. Start telling a story—it can be about anything you can think of. Stories are especially fun if the child is one of the characters in them. Once you've been talking for a minute or so, stop and let your grandchild take over. When he or she starts to get stuck, you take over again. Don't worry about getting the story perfect—just be imaginative and see where it takes you!

If you want, write down the story in a blank book and let your grandchild illustrate it. Then you can enjoy it together over and over!

Plant Something!

HELP the little ones develop a green thumb with a simple planting project! Not only can planting be lots of fun, but if kids help grow their own fruits and vegetables, they're much more likely to eat them. To make planting even more exciting, choose creative containers—try a shoe the kids have grown out of (Crocs are great, since they have holes for drainage, and rubber boots work well), a wicker basket, or a child's swimming pool. If the container doesn't have holes for drainage, make sure you can poke or drill some.

You will need:

> Potting soil
> Planting container
> Seeds

Directions:

1. Decide what you'd like to plant together. Choose something that grows easily in containers, such as basil, oregano, strawberries, lettuce, carrots, pansies, impatiens, or sweet alyssum.

2. Fill your container about three quarters full with potting soil and follow the instructions on the seed packet for planting.

3. Place the pot somewhere where it will get plenty of sunlight, and water regularly.

"Cooking is at once child's play and adult joy. And cooking done with care is an act of love."

~Craig Claiborne

Recipes

Chocolate Fudge

THE ultimate sweet indulgence, fudge will turn any sweet tooth into a big grin. This recipe is easy enough for the kids to do themselves with just a little supervision.

Makes 2 pounds of fudge

Ingredients:

1 (14-ounce) can sweetened condensed milk
1 (12-ounce) package semisweet chocolate chips
2 tablespoons butter
1 teaspoon vanilla

Directions:

1. Grease a 9-inch square pan.

2. Heat all the ingredients in a double boiler, stirring until the chocolate chips are fully melted and the mixture is smooth.

3. Pour into the greased pan and chill until firm.

"Families are like fudge, mostly sweet with a few nuts."

~Unknown

Homemade Ice Cream

DON'T have an ice cream maker? Don't let that stop you from making this classic summer treat. This method is more fun than using an electric ice cream maker, anyway. If desired, at the end you can add cocoa powder, chopped strawberries, crushed peppermint sticks, or other candy or fruit.

Makes 1 pint

Supplies:

One-pound coffee can
Three-pound coffee can
Duct tape

Ice
1 cup salt

Ingredients:

2 cups half-and-half
½ cup sugar

1 teaspoon vanilla

Direction:

1. Mix all the ingredients in the one-pound coffee can. Cover the lid with duct tape to ensure it is tightly sealed.

2. Place the smaller can inside the larger can and fill the space between the two with ice and salt.

3. Cover the large can and seal with duct tape. Roll the can back and forth for 15 minutes. To reduce noise, place a towel on your work surface, or work on a rug.

4. Dump out ice and water. Stir the contents of the small can. Store ice cream in a glass or plastic container (if you leave it in the can it may take on a metallic flavor).

"I figured if I was going to make the world a better place, I'd do it with cookies."

~Ana Pascal, "Stranger than Fiction"

Chocolate-Peanut Butter Crunch Bars

THESE tasty bars are great to take along for a picnic or a hike through the woods.

Makes about 30 small bars

Ingredients:

1 (16-ounce) package semisweet chocolate chips

½ cup peanut butter chips

⅓ cup butter

1 teaspoon vanilla

2 cups crisp rice cereal

1 cup quick-cooking rolled oats

Glaze:

¼ cup peanut butter chips

1 teaspoon oil

Directions:

1. Grease a 9-inch square or round pan. In a microwave-safe bowl, combine chocolate chips, ½ cup peanut butter chips, and butter. Microwave on medium heat for 2–3 minutes, stirring halfway through cooking. Stir until smooth. Stir in vanilla. Add cereal and oats and stir until well coated. Press in greased pan.

2. To prepare glaze, combine peanut butter chips and oil in a small microwave-safe bowl. Microwave on medium for 1–2 minutes. Stir until smooth. Drizzle over bars. Refrigerate until set. Cut into bars.

Food Art

SOMETIMES it's okay to play with your food—especially if it helps kids enjoy healthy snacks. For this recipe, provide the kids with the ingredients and let them create their own artful treats. If they're looking for inspiration, suggest making butterflies, caterpillars, trucks, monsters, people, flowers, hearts, or letters to "write" their names with.

Building Blocks:

Carrot, celery, zucchini, or cucumber sticks; apple, banana, orange, kiwi, mango, or pineapple slices; melon balls; lettuce or spinach leaves; sliced lunch meat or cheese

Glue:

Peanut butter (or other nut butter), cream cheese, cottage cheese, or yogurt

Finishing Touches:

Nuts, seeds, raisins, radish slices, shredded carrots, berries, cherries, ketchup

"Few things are more delightful than grandchildren fighting over your lap."

~Doug Larson

"Nobody can do for little children what grandparents do. Grandparents sort of sprinkle stardust over the lives of little children."

~Alex Haley

Chocolate-Peppermint Spoons

THESE festive treats are great for stirring hot cocoa or just for enjoying like a lollipop!

Makes 20 spoons

Ingredients:

1 cup chocolate chips   20 plastic spoons
5 candy canes

Directions:

1. Line a baking sheet with aluminum foil. Crush the candy canes by pulsing them in a food processor or placing them in a plastic bag and rolling a glass or a rolling pin over it.

2. Melt the chocolate chips in a double boiler or in the microwave, stirring regularly until smooth.

3. Dip each spoon in the melted chocolate and then sprinkle a layer of the crushed candy canes over the chocolate. Place the spoons on the baking sheet and refrigerate for about 15 minutes or until set. Store in the refrigerator in an airtight container.

Lemonade

WHAT'S more refreshing than old-fashioned homemade lemonade? Enjoy the classic version or spruce it up with one of the variations below.

Makes about 4 servings

Ingredients:

Juice from 4 lemons   ½ cup sugar
1 quart water

Directions:

1. Combine all ingredients in a large pitcher and chill.

Fun Variations:

- Make it hot pink! Add ½ cup fresh or frozen blueberries and stir until the liquid becomes pink.

- Make it fizzy! Add 1 cup of seltzer and stir gently.

- Make it fruity! In a blender, combine the lemonade with a handful of strawberries, some chopped watermelon, and/or raspberries and whir until smooth.

Macaroni and Cheese

THERE are lots of fancy recipes for macaroni and cheese available online and in foodie magazines, but I'm still partial to the way my mother and my grandmother always made it. It's put together more like lasagna, with layers of noodles and cheese—it's easy, quick, and still one of my all-time favorite meals.

Makes about 6 servings

Ingredients:

1 one-pound box elbow macaroni

2 cups (½ pound) sharp cheddar cheese

1 cup milk or light cream

Salt and pepper to taste

Potato chips (optional)

Directions:

1. Preheat oven to 350°F. Bring 4 quarters of salted water to a boil and cook the macaroni until tender. Drain. Thinly slice or grate the cheese.

2. Place a layer of cooked macaroni in a 1½-quart casserole dish. Top with a layer of cheese, then another layer of macaroni. Repeat, ending with a thick layer of cheese. Drizzle the milk or cream over the top. Bake for about 20 minutes, adding crushed potato chips as a thin top layer after about 10 minutes, if desired.

Hot Chocolate with Homemade Marshmallows

HOMEMADE hot chocolate is a treat that is sure to make the little ones feel warm and fuzzy all over. The homemade marshmallows are an extra special touch.

Makes 5 servings

Ingredients:

4 cups milk

½ cup sugar

¼ cup baking cocoa

$\frac{1}{8}$ teaspoon salt

1 teaspoon vanilla extract

Directions:

1. In a saucepan, combine ½ cup milk, sugar, cocoa, and salt and stir over medium-low heat until dissolved.

2. Add remaining milk and continue to heat and stir until steaming.

3. Remove from heat and whisk in vanilla. Pour into mugs, add marshmallows (recipe follows), and serve.

Homemade Marshmallows

IF you've never tasted homemade marshmallows, you are missing out. Fluffy and delicately sweet, they are a divine treat. Make this recipe at least one day before you plan to indulge in them.

Makes about 24 (2½-inch) marshmallows

Ingredients:

1 cup cold water
3 envelopes (3 tablespoons)
   unflavored gelatin
2 cups sugar

¾ cup light corn syrup
¼ teaspoon salt
1 teaspoon vanilla
Confectioners' sugar

Directions:

1. Line a 9 x 13 x 2-inch pan with parchment paper and dust the paper with about 3 tablespoons of confectioners' sugar.

2. Pour ½ cup cold water in a bowl, sprinkle the gelatin over the water, and let rest for about 15 minutes.

3. Meanwhile, heat the other ½ cup water, sugar, salt, and corn syrup in a 2-quart saucepan over medium heat, stirring until the sugar dissolves and the mixture comes to a boil.

4. Cover and allow to boil for about 3 minutes to dissolve any sugar crystals on the sides of the pan.

5. Remove the lid, turn up the heat, insert a candy thermometer, and don't stir until the temperature reaches 240°F. Remove from the heat.

6. Use an electric beater at medium speed to begin beating the gelatin and water mixture, adding the syrup in a slow, thin stream. Once added, increase the speed to high and beat for another 10 minutes. The mixture will turn white, fluffy, and sticky. Add the vanilla and beat another minute or so to combine.

7. Scoop the marshmallow fluff into the prepared pan, using a damp spatula to spread it as smoothly as possible. Dust the top with another 3 tablespoons confectioners' sugar. Set in a cool, dry place and allow to sit uncovered for 12 hours.

8. To remove the marshmallows from the pan, run a knife around the edges of the pan to loosen the marshmallows. Then invert the pan onto a cutting board dusted with more confectioners' sugar. Peel off the parchment paper and cut the marshmallows into squares. Store in an airtight container for up to two weeks.

"What children need most are the essentials that grandparents provide in abundance. They give unconditional love, kindness, patience, humor, comfort, lessons in life. And, most importantly, cookies."

~Rudolph Giuliani

Oatmeal Chocolate Chip Cookies

THESE cookies are perfect for taking on a hike—or for an energy booster when the kids start to wear you out!

Makes about 3 dozen cookies

Ingredients:

1½ cups rolled oats
1 stick unsalted butter, at room temperature
½ cup sugar
½ cup brown sugar, firmly packed
1 egg

1 teaspoon vanilla extract
1 cup all-purpose flour
½ teaspoon baking powder
½ teaspoon baking soda
¼ teaspoon salt
1 bag semisweet chocolate chips

Directions:

1. Preheat the oven to 375°F.

2. Place 1¼ cups of the oats in a food processor and process until fine, about 1 minute.

3. Beat the butter with both sugars in the large bowl of an electric mixer until smooth. Beat in the egg and vanilla.

4. Combine the processed oats with the flour, baking powder, baking soda, and salt. Slowly add to the butter mixture. Then stir in the remaining ¼ cup oats and the chocolate chips.

5. Drop the dough by spoonfuls onto ungreased baking sheets and bake until golden brown, about 10 minutes. Cool slightly on the sheets before removing.

"The most indispensable ingredient of all good home cooking: love, for those you are cooking for."
~Sophia Loren

Popcorn Balls

PERFECT for Christmas, Halloween, or really anytime, popcorn balls are lots of fun for kids to make. Let them use their little hands to form the sticky and delicious balls—it's okay for cooking to get a little messy sometimes.

Makes about 12 medium-sized balls

Ingredients:

½ cup popping corn or one bag microwave popcorn
½ teaspoon salt
½ cup maple or dark corn syrup

½ cup sugar
½ teaspoon vanilla
2 tablespoons butter

Directions:

1. Pop the popcorn according to instructions and place in a large bowl.

2. Heat the syrup, sugar, vanilla, and butter in a large saucepan, stirring regularly. Allow to boil for 2 minutes. Pour over the popcorn and mix with a spoon.

3. Allow popcorn to cool for a few minutes as you coat your hands with butter or oil. Form balls, using about 1 cup of popcorn for each ball. Place on waxed paper and allow to cool.

• For fun variations, mix in 1 cup mini marshmallows or M&Ms just before forming balls, or add ½ cup peanut butter to the syrup mixture before pouring over the popped popcorn.

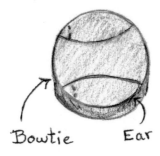

Bowtie   Ear

Rabbit Cake

HERE'S a fun cake to make for Easter or anytime!

You will need:

- 2 round cake layers
- Cutting board and knife
- Vanilla frosting
- Dried shredded coconut
- Maraschino cherries

Directions:

1. One cake layer will be the rabbit's face. This one doesn't need to be cut. Cut the other layer into ears and a bowtie as shown.

2. Put the pieces in place on a cutting board and frost. Dust with the dried coconut for "fur." Cut a maraschino cherry in half for eyes. Use a knife to "draw" whiskers in the frosting. Frost the inside of the ears with pink frosting.

"Grandmas are moms with lots of frosting."
~Anonymous

Velvety Chocolate Cupcakes

YOU may notice that this is, essentially, a red velvet cupcake recipe without the red. Most red velvet cupcake recipes call for two bottles of food coloring. Now I realize sugar and butter may not be the healthiest ingredients to feed the kiddies, but, justified or not, the thought of that much food coloring makes me cringe way more. These cupcakes are moist, rich, and a lovely natural shade of cocoa-brown.

Makes 2 dozen cupcakes

Ingredients:

1 teaspoon baking soda	3 tablespoons cocoa
1 tablespoon vinegar	1 teaspoon vanilla
½ cup unsalted butter, softened	1 cup buttermilk
1½ cups sugar	2¼ cups flour
2 eggs	1 teaspoon salt

Directions:

1. Preheat oven to 350°F. Line two 12-cup muffin tins with cupcake liners.

2. Mix vinegar and baking soda in a medium bowl (it will get fizzy, so don't use a bowl that's very shallow). Set aside. Cream sugar, butter, and eggs until light. Add the cocoa and mix.

3. In a small bowl or measuring cup, combine buttermilk and vanilla. Combine salt and flour in a separate small bowl.

Continued on next page . . .

4. Add the buttermilk mixture and the flour mixture alternately to the butter mixture, ending with the flour mixture. Add baking soda and vinegar mixture to batter. Mix just until blended.

5. Divide batter between the prepared pans, and bake for about 30 minutes or until the tops of the cupcakes are springy when lightly touched.

6. Cool completely before frosting.

Cream Cheese Frosting:

1. In a large bowl, combine ¼ cup softened butter, 1 package (8 ounces) cream cheese, 1 pound confectioners sugar, and 2 teaspoons vanilla extract. Beat until smooth.

Mini Pizzas

WHAT kid doesn't love pizza? English muffin halves make easy crusts in this recipe. Let kids "decorate" their own pizzas with their favorite toppings. Making pizza faces is especially fun—olives make great eyes, red pepper strips are perfect lips and pepperoni slices make lovely rosy cheeks.

Ingredients:

2 English muffin halves per person   Toppings, such as pepperoni,
Pizza sauce   sliced green or red peppers,
Shredded mozzarella cheese   olives, broccoli, fresh basil, etc.

Directions:

1. Preheat the oven to 375°F.

2. Place the English muffin halves cut side up on a baking sheet. Spread a couple tablespoons of pizza sauce over each half. Sprinkle cheese, toppings, and a little more cheese on top.

3. Bake for about 10 minutes or until the cheese is bubbly and golden. Allow to cool a few minutes before serving.

Peter Rabbit's Favorite Salad

MANY people assume kids won't eat obviously healthy dishes. If you're one of those people, prove yourself wrong by making this yummy salad full of carrots, just like Peter Rabbit would like it! Slightly sweet and with plenty of crunch, this salad is quick to make and quick to disappear.

4–6 servings

Ingredients:

1 pound carrots, peeled and grated
2 firm apples, cored and chopped
1 cup crushed pineapple, drained
2 tablespoons orange juice
⅓ cup mayonnaise
½ teaspoon salt
⅓ cup raisins or dried cranberries

Directions:

1. Combine all ingredients in a large bowl.

2. Refrigerate until scrving.

"Vegetables are a must on a diet. I suggest carrot cake, zucchini bread, and pumpkin pie."

~Jim Davis

Stories and Nursery Rhymes

Baa, baa, black sheep,
Have you any wool?
Yes, marry, have I,
Three bags full;
One for my master,
And one for my dame,
And one for the little boy
Who lives down the lane.

The Elves and the Shoemaker

Adapted from the Grimm Brothers' tale

There was once a shoemaker, who, through no fault of his own, became so poor that at last he had nothing left but just enough leather to make one pair of shoes. He cut out the shoes at night so he could start sewing them first thing the next morning and then went to bed and fell sound asleep. In the morning, after he had said his prayers, he was about to get to work when he found the pair of shoes already finished and sitting on his table! He was very much astonished, and didn't know what to think, and he picked the shoes up to examine them more closely. They were so well made that every stitch was in its right place, just as if they had come from the hand of a master-workman.

Soon after, a customer entered his shop and tried on the shoes. They fit him so well that he gave the shoemaker more than the usual price for them, so that the shoemaker had enough money to buy leather for two more pairs of shoes. He cut them out at night, and intended to set to work the next morning with fresh spirit; but that was not to be, for when he got up they were already finished, and right away a customer came in, tried on the shoes, and gave the shoemaker so much money that he was able to buy leather enough for four new pairs.

Early the next morning he found the four pairs also finished, and so it happened every day; whatever he cut out in the evening was finished by the morning, so that soon he was making a good living, and in the end became very well-to-do.

One night, not long before Christmas, when the shoemaker had finished cutting out, and before he went to bed, he said to his wife, "Perhaps we should stay awake tonight and discover who is doing all this work for us." His wife agreed, and lit a candle to burn all night. Then they hid in a corner of the room, behind some coats that were hanging up, and they began to watch. As soon as it was midnight they saw come in two tiny men in very thin and ragged clothes, who seated themselves at the shoemaker's table, took up the work that was already prepared, and began to stitch, and pierce, and to hammer so cleverly and quickly with their little fingers that the shoemaker's eyes could scarcely follow them. They never took a break until everything was finished and was standing ready on the table. Then they jumped up and ran off.

The next morning the shoemaker's wife said to her husband, "Those little men have made us rich, and we ought to show them how grateful we are. With all their running about in those old ragged clothes, they must be very cold. I tell you what: I will make little shirts, coats, and pants for them, and knit each of them a pair of stockings, and you can make each of them a pair of shoes."

The husband agreed happily, and at night, when everything was finished, they laid the gifts together on the table instead of the cut-out work, and again hid in a corner so they could watch what the little men would do. When midnight came, they rushed in, ready to set to work, but when they found, instead of the pieces of prepared leather, the new little garments set out for them, they stood a moment in surprise, and then they began to laugh and hug each other and skip about with glee. Quickly they took the pretty garments and slipped them on, singing,

"What spruce and dandy boys are we!
No longer cobblers we will be."

Then they hopped and danced about, jumping over the chairs and tables, and at last they danced out the door.

After that night they were never seen again; but they had helped the shoemaker so much that his shop flourished for as long as he lived and he and his wife never forgot the elves who had made their lives so much happier.

Jack and Jill
Went up the hill,
To fetch a pail of water;
Jack fell down
And broke his crown,
And Jill came tumbling after.

Little Bo-Peep has lost
her sheep,
And can't tell where to
find them;
Leave them alone, and
they'll come home,
And bring their tails
behind them.

The Princess and the Pea

Adapted from Hans Christian Anderson's tale

Once upon a time there was a prince who wanted to marry, but he was only allowed to marry a real princess. He traveled all over the world, but nowhere could he find a suitable princess to be his wife. There were princesses enough, but it was difficult to find out whether they were real ones. There was always something about them that was not as it should be. So he came home again and was very sad, beginning to think he would be lonely for the rest of his life.

One evening a terrible storm came on; there was thunder and lightning, and the rain poured down in torrents. Suddenly a knocking was heard at the city gate, and the old king went to open it.

It was a princess standing out there in front of the gate. But, good gracious! What a sight the rain and the wind had made her look. The water ran down from her hair and clothes; it ran down into the toes of her shoes and out again at the heels. And yet she said that she was a real princess.

The old queen didn't think she looked much like a princess at all. "Well, we'll soon find out," she thought. But she said nothing, went into the bedroom, took all the bedding off the bedstead, and laid a pea on the bottom; then she took twenty mattresses and laid them on the pea, and then laid twenty thick quilts on top of the mattresses.

On this the princess had to lie all night. In the morning she was asked how she had slept.

The princess hesitated to answer, not wanting to be rude. But after the queen asked her twice more, she said, as politely as possible, "Not very well, I'm afraid. Though you made me a lovely bed, I still felt as though I were lying on something hard. It was very strange!"

Now they knew that she was a real princess because she had felt the pea right through the twenty mattresses and the twenty thick quilts.

Nobody but a real princess could be as sensitive as that.

So the prince took her for his wife, and the pea was put in the museum, where it may still be seen, if no one has stolen it.

Little Miss Muffet,
Sat on a tuffet,
Eating some curds and whey;
There came a great spider,
And sat down beside her,
And frightened Miss Muffet away.

The north wind doth blow,
And we shall have snow,
And what will poor Robin do then?
Poor thing!

He'll sit in a barn,
And to keep himself warm,
Will hide his head under his wing,
Poor thing!

The Ugly Duckling

Adapted from Hans Christian Andersen's tale

It was lovely summer weather in the country, and the golden corn, the green oats, and the haystacks piled up in the meadows looked beautiful. The stork walking about on his long red legs chattered in the Egyptian language, which he had learnt from his mother. The cornfields and meadows were surrounded by large forests, in the midst of which were deep pools. It was, indeed, delightful to walk about in the country. In a sunny spot stood a pleasant old farmhouse close by a deep river, and from the house down to the waterside grew great burdock leaves, so high that under the tallest of them a little child could stand upright. The spot was as wild as the center of a thick wood. In this snug retreat sat a duck on her nest, watching for her young brood to hatch; she was beginning to get tired of her task, for the little ones were a long time coming out of their shells, and she seldom had any visitors. The other ducks liked much better to swim about in the river than to climb the slippery banks, and sit under a burdock leaf, to gossip with her. At length one shell cracked, and then another, and from each egg came a living creature that lifted its head and cried, "Peep, peep." "Quack, quack," said the mother, and then they all quacked as well as they could, and looked about them on every side at the large green leaves. Their mother allowed them to look as much as they liked, because green is good for the eyes. "How large the world is," said the young ducks, when they found how much more room they now had than while they were inside the eggshell. "Do you imagine this is the whole world?" asked the mother; "Wait till you have seen the garden; it stretches far beyond that to the parson's field, but I have never ventured to such a distance. Are you all out?" she continued, rising; "No, I declare, the largest egg lies there still. I wonder how long this is to last, I am quite tired of it;" and she seated herself again on the nest.

"Well, how are you getting on?" asked an old duck, who paid her a visit.

"One egg is not hatched yet," said the duck, "it will not break. But just look at all the others, are they not the prettiest little ducklings you ever saw? They are the image of their father, who is so unkind, he never comes to see."

"Let me see the egg that will not break," said the duck, "I have no doubt it is a turkey's egg. I was persuaded to hatch some once, and after all my care and trouble with the young ones, they were afraid of the water. I quacked and clucked, but all to no purpose. I could not get them to venture in. Let me look at the egg. Yes, that is a turkey's egg; take my advice, leave it where it is and teach the other children to swim."

"I think I will sit on it a little while longer," said the duck, "as I have sat so long already, a few days will be nothing."

"Please yourself," said the old duck, and she went away.

At last the large egg broke, and a young one crept forth crying, "Peep, peep." It was very large and ugly. The duck stared at it and exclaimed, "It is very large and not at all like the others. I wonder if it really is a turkey. We shall soon find it out, however, when we go to the water. It must go in, if I have to push it myself."

On the next day the weather was delightful, and the sun shone brightly on the green burdock leaves, so the mother duck took her young brood down to the water, and jumped in with a splash. "Quack, quack," she cried, and one after another the little ducklings jumped in. The water closed over their heads, but they came up again in an instant, and swam about quite prettily with their legs paddling under them as easily as possible, and the ugly duckling was also in the water swimming with them.

"Oh," said the mother, "that is not a turkey; how well he uses his legs, and how upright he holds himself! He is my own child, and he is not so very ugly after all if you look at him properly. Quack, quack! come with me now, I will take you into grand society, and introduce you to the farmyard, but you must keep close to me or you may be trodden upon; and, above all, beware of the cat."

When they reached the farmyard, there was a great disturbance; two families were fighting for an eel's head, which, after all, was carried off by the cat. "See, children, that is the way of the world," said the mother duck, whetting her beak, for she would have liked the eel's head herself. "Come, now, use your legs, and let me see how well you can behave. You must bow your heads prettily to that old duck yonder; she is the highest born of them all. Don't you see she has a red flag tied to her leg, which is something very grand, and a great honor for a duck; it shows that everyone is anxious not to lose her, as she can be recognized both by man and beast. Come, now, don't turn your toes, a well-bred duckling spreads his feet wide apart, just like his father and mother, in this way; now bend your neck, and say 'quack.'"

The ducklings did as they were bid, but one spiteful duck who was watching said, "Look, here comes another brood, as if there were not enough of us already! and what a queer-looking object one of them is; we don't want him here," and then bit him on the neck.

"Let him alone," said the mother, "he is not doing any harm."

"Yes, but he is so big and ugly," said the spiteful duck, "and therefore he must be turned out."

"The others are very pretty children," said the old duck with the rag on her leg, "all but that one; I wish his mother could improve him a little."

"That is impossible, your grace," replied the mother "he is not pretty; but he has a very good disposition, and swims as well or even better than the others. I think he will grow up pretty, and perhaps be smaller; he has remained too long in the egg, and therefore his figure is not properly formed," and then she stroked his neck and smoothed the feathers, saying, "It is a drake, and therefore not of so much consequence. I think he will grow up strong, and able to take care of himself."

"The other ducklings are graceful enough," said the old duck. "Now make yourself at home, and if you can find an eel's head, you can bring it to me."

And so they made themselves comfortable; but the poor duckling, who had crept out of his shell last of all, and looked so ugly, was bitten and pushed and made fun of, not only by the ducks, but by all the poultry. "He is too big," they all said, and the turkey cock, who had been born into the world with spurs, and fancied himself really an emperor, puffed himself out like a vessel in full sail, and flew at the duckling, and became quite red in the head with passion, so that the poor little thing did not know where to go, and was quite miserable because he was so ugly and laughed at by the whole farmyard. So it went on from day to day till it got worse and worse. The poor duckling was driven about by everyone; even his brothers and sisters were unkind to him, and would say, "Ah, you ugly creature, I wish the cat would get you," and his mother felt so sorry for him that even she began to wish he had never been born. The ducks pecked him, the chickens beat him, and the girl who fed the poultry kicked him with her feet. So at last he ran away, frightening the little birds in the hedge as he flew over the palings.

"They are afraid of me because I am ugly," he said. So he closed his eyes, and flew still farther, until he came out on a large moor, inhabited by wild ducks. Here he remained the whole night, feeling very tired and sorrowful.

In the morning, when the wild ducks rose in the air, they stared at their new comrade. "What sort of a duck are you?" they all said, coming round him.

He bowed to them, and was as polite as he could be, but he did not reply to their question. "You are exceedingly ugly," said the wild ducks, "but that will not matter if you do not want to marry one of our family."

Poor thing! he had no thoughts of marriage; all he wanted was permission to lie among the rushes, and drink some of the water on the moor. After he had been on the moor two days, there came two wild geese, or rather goslings, for they had not been out of the egg long, and were very saucy. "Listen, friend," said one of them to the duckling, "you are so ugly, that we like you very well. Will you go with us, and become a bird of passage? Not far from here is another moor, in which there are some pretty wild geese, all unmarried. It is a chance for you to get a wife; you may be lucky, ugly as you are."

Just then "pop, pop," sounded in the air, and the two wild geese squawked "Fly away, quick!" "Pop, pop," echoed far and wide in the distance, and whole flocks of wild geese rose up from the rushes. The sound continued from every direction, for the sportsmen surrounded the moor, and some were even seated on branches of trees, overlooking the rushes. The blue smoke from the guns rose like clouds over the dark trees, and as it floated away across the water, a number of sporting dogs bounded in among the rushes, which bent beneath them wherever they went. How they terrified the poor duckling, who had never heard such a noise before and had been too startled to fly away with the others! He turned away his head to hide it under his wing, and at the same moment a large terrible dog passed quite near him. His jaws were open, his tongue hung from his mouth, and his eyes glared fearfully. He thrust his nose close to the duckling, showing his sharp teeth, and then, "splash, splash," he went into the water without touching him. "Oh," sighed the duckling, "how thankful I am for being so ugly; even a dog will not bite me." And so he lay quite still, while the shots rattled through the rushes, and gun after gun was fired over him. It was late in the day before all became quiet, but even then the poor young thing did not dare to move. He waited quietly for several hours, and then, after looking carefully around him, hastened away from the moor as fast as he could. He ran over field and meadow till a storm arose, and he could hardly struggle against it. Towards evening, he reached a poor little cottage that seemed ready to fall, and only remained standing because it could not decide on which side to fall first. The storm continued so violently, that the duckling could go no farther; he sat down by the cottage, and then he noticed that the door was not quite closed because one of the hinges had given way. There was a narrow opening near the bottom large enough for him to slip through, which he did very quietly, and got a shelter for the night. A woman, a tom cat, and a hen lived in this cottage. The tom cat, whom the mistress called, "My little son," was a great favorite; he could raise his back, and purr, and could even throw out sparks from his fur if it were stroked the wrong way. The hen had very short legs, so she was called "Chickie short legs." She laid good eggs, and her mistress loved her as if she had been her own child. In the morning, the strange visitor was discovered, and the tom cat began to purr, and the hen to cluck.

"What is that noise about?" said the old woman, looking round the room, but her sight was not very good, when she saw the duckling she thought it must be a fat duck, that had strayed from home. "Oh what a prize!" she exclaimed, "I hope it is not a drake, for then I shall have some duck's eggs. I must wait and see." So the duckling was allowed to remain on trial for three weeks, but there were no eggs. Now the tom cat was the master of the house, and the hen was mistress, and they always said, "We and the world," for they believed themselves to be half the world, and the better half, too. The duckling thought that others might hold a different opinion on the subject, but the hen would not listen to such doubts. "Can you lay eggs?" she asked. "No." "Then have the goodness to hold your tongue." "Can you raise your back, or purr, or throw out sparks?" said the tom cat. "No." "Then you have no right to express an opinion when sensible creatures are speaking." So the duckling sat in a corner, feeling very low spirited, till the sunshine and the fresh air came into the room through the open door, and then he began to feel such a great longing for a swim on the water, that he could not help telling the hen.

"What an absurd idea," said the hen. "You have nothing else to do, therefore you have foolish fancies. If you could purr or lay eggs, they would pass away."

"But it is so delightful to swim about on the water," said the duckling, "and so refreshing to feel it close over your head, while you dive down to the bottom."

"Delightful, indeed!" said the hen, "why you must be crazy! Ask the cat, he is the cleverest animal I know. Ask him how he would like to swim about on the water, or to dive under it, for I will not speak of my own opinion; ask our mistress, the old woman—there is no one in the world more clever than she is. Do you think she would like to swim, or to let the water close over her head?"

"You don't understand me," said the duckling.

"We don't understand you? Who can understand you, I wonder? Do you consider yourself more clever than the cat, or the old woman? I will say nothing of myself. Don't imagine such nonsense, child, and thank your good fortune that you have been received here. Are you not in a warm room, and in society from which you may learn something? But you are a chatterer, and your company is not very agreeable. Believe me, I speak only for your own good. I may tell you unpleasant truths, but that is a proof of my friendship. I advise you, therefore, to lay eggs, and learn to purr as quickly as possible."

"I believe I must go out into the world again," said the duckling.

"Yes, do," said the hen. So the duckling left the cottage, and soon found water on which it could swim and dive, but was avoided by all other animals, because of its ugly appearance. Autumn came, and the leaves in the forest turned to orange and gold. Then, as winter approached, the wind caught them as they fell and whirled them in the cold air. The clouds, heavy with hail and snowflakes, hung low in the sky, and the raven stood on the ferns crying, "Croak, croak." It made one shiver with cold to look at him. All this was very sad for the poor little duckling. One evening, just as the sun set amid radiant clouds, there came a large flock of beautiful birds out of the bushes. The duckling had never seen any like them before. They were swans, and they curved their graceful necks, while their soft plumage shown with dazzling whiteness. They uttered a singular cry, as they spread their glorious wings and flew away from those cold regions to warmer countries across the sea. As they mounted higher and higher in the air, the ugly little duckling felt quite a strange sensation as he watched them. He whirled himself in the water like a wheel, stretched out his neck towards them, and uttered a cry so strange that he frightened himself. Could he ever forget those beautiful, happy birds? When at last they were out of his sight, he dived under the water, and rose again almost beside himself with excitement. He knew not the names of these birds, nor where they had flown, but he felt towards them as he had never felt for any other bird in the world. He was not envious of these beautiful creatures, but wished to be as lovely as they. Poor ugly creature, how gladly he would have lived even with the ducks had they only given him encouragement. The winter grew colder and colder; he was obliged to swim about on the water to keep it from freezing, but every night the space on which he swam became smaller and smaller. At length it froze so hard that the ice in the water crackled as he moved, and the duckling had to paddle with his legs as well as he could, to keep the space from closing up. He became exhausted at last, and lay still and helpless, frozen fast in the ice.

Early in the morning, a peasant, who was passing by, saw what had happened. He broke the ice in pieces with his wooden shoe, and carried the duckling home to his wife. The warmth revived the poor little creature; but when the children wanted to play with him, the duckling thought they would do him some harm; so he started up in terror, fluttered into the milk-pan, and splashed the milk about the room. Then the woman clapped her hands, which frightened him still more. He flew first into the butter-cask, then into the meal-tub, and out again. What a condition he was in! The woman screamed, and struck at him with the tongs; the children laughed and screamed, and tumbled over each other, in their efforts to catch him; but luckily he escaped. The door stood open; the poor creature could just manage to slip out among the bushes, and lie down quite exhausted in the newly fallen snow.

When the winter had finally passed, the dukcling found himself lying one morning in a moor, amongst the rushes. He felt the warm sun shining, and heard the lark singing, and saw that all around was beautiful spring. Then the young bird felt that his wings were strong, as he flapped them against his sides, and rose high into the air. They bore him onwards, until he found himself in a large garden, before he knew how it had happened. The apple trees were in full blossom, and the fragrant elders bent their long green branches down to the stream which wound round a smooth lawn. Everything looked beautiful, in the freshness of early spring. From a thicket close by came three beautiful white swans, rustling their feathers, and swimming lightly over the smooth water. The duckling remembered the lovely birds, and felt more strangely unhappy than ever.

"I will fly to those royal birds," he exclaimed, "and they will kill me, because I am so ugly, and dare to approach them; but it does not matter: better be killed by them than pecked by the ducks, beaten by the hens, pushed about by the maiden who feeds the poultry, or starved with hunger in the winter."

Then he flew to the water, and swam towards the beautiful swans. The moment they espied the stranger, they rushed to meet him with outstretched wings.

The duckling bent his head down to the surface of the water, and waited to see what they would do.

But what did he see in the clear stream below? His own image; no longer a dark, gray bird, ugly and disagreeable to look at, but a graceful and beautiful swan. To be born in a duck's nest, in a farmyard, is of no consequence to a bird, if it is hatched from a swan's egg. He now felt glad at having suffered sorrow and trouble, because it enabled him to enjoy so much better all the pleasure and happiness around him; for the great swans swam round the new-comer, and stroked his neck with their beaks, as a welcome.

Into the garden presently came some little children, who threw bread and cake into the water.

"See," cried the youngest, "there is a new one," and the rest were delighted, and ran to their father and mother, dancing and clapping their hands, and shouting joyously, "There is another swan come; a new one has arrived."

Then they threw more bread and cake into the water, and said, "The new one is the most beautiful of all; he is so young and pretty." And the old swans bowed their heads before him.

Then he felt quite ashamed, and hid his head under his wing; for he did not know what to do, he was so happy, and yet not at all proud. He had been despised for his ugliness, and now he heard them say he was the most beautiful of all the birds. Even the elder-tree bent down its bows into the water before him, and the sun shone warm and bright. Then he rustled his feathers, curved his slender neck, and cried joyfully, from the depths of his heart, "I never dreamed of such happiness as this, while I was an ugly duckling."

Pat-a-cake,
Pat-a-cake,
Baker's man!
So I will, master, as fast as I can:
Pat it, and prick it, and mark it with T,
Put it in the oven for Tommy and me.

The Twelve Dancing Princesses

Adapted from the Grimm Brothers' tale

There once was a king who had twelve beautiful daughters. They slept in twelve beds all in one room and when they went to bed, the doors were shut and locked up. However, every morning their shoes were found to be quite worn through as if they had been danced in all night. Nobody could find out how it happened, or where the princesses had been.

So the king made it known to all the land that if any person could discover the secret and find out where it was that the princesses danced in the night, he could ask the one he liked best to be his wife, and would be king after his death. But whoever tried and did not succeed, after three days and nights, would be thrown out of the kingdom.

A king's son soon came. He was well entertained, and in the evening was taken to the chamber next to the one where the princesses lay in their twelve beds. There he was to sit and watch where they went to dance; and, in order that nothing could happen without him hearing it, the door of his chamber was left open. But the king's son soon fell asleep, and when he awoke in the morning he found that the princesses had all been dancing, for the soles of their shoes were full of holes.

The same thing happened the second and third night and so the prince failed.

After him came several others; but they all had the same luck, and all were thrown out of the kingdom.

Now it happened that an old soldier, who had been wounded in battle and could fight no longer, passed through the country where this king reigned, and as he was traveling through a forest, he met an old woman, who asked him where he was going.

"I hardly know where I am going, or what I should do," said the soldier; "but I think I would like to find out where it is that the princesses dance, and then in time I might become king."

"Well," said the old woman, "that is not so difficult. But take care not to drink any of the wine which one of the princesses will bring to you in the evening, and as soon as she leaves you, pretend to be fast asleep."

Then she gave him a cloak, and said, "As soon as you put this cloak on you will become invisible, and you will then be able to follow the princesses wherever they go." When the soldier heard all this good advice, he was determined to try his luck, so he went to the king, and said he was willing to undertake the task.

He was as well received as the others had been, and the king ordered fine royal robes to be given him; and when the evening came he was led to the outer chamber.

Just as he was going to lie down, the eldest of the princesses brought him a cup of wine, but the soldier threw it all away secretly, taking care not to drink a drop. Then he lay down on his bed, and in a little while began to snore very loudly as if he was fast asleep.

When the twelve princesses heard this they laughed heartily; and the eldest said, "Poor fool! Soon, he, too, shall be cast out of the kingdom." Then they rose and opened their drawers and boxes, and took out all their fine clothes, and dressed themselves at the mirror, and skipped about as if they were eager to begin dancing.

But the youngest said, "I don't know why it is, but while you are so happy I feel very uneasy; I am sure some mischance will befall us."

"Don't be silly," said the eldest, "you are always afraid; have you forgotten how many kings' sons have already watched in vain? And as for this soldier, even if I had not given him his sleeping draught, he would have slept soundly enough."

When they were all ready, they went and looked at the soldier; but he snored on, and did not move even a finger, so they thought they were quite safe.

Then the eldest went up to her own bed and clapped her hands, and the bed sank into the floor and a trap-door flew open. The soldier saw them going down through the trap-door one after another, the eldest leading the way and, thinking he had no time to lose, he jumped up, put on the cloak which the old woman had given him, and followed them.

However, in the middle of the stairs he trod on the gown of the youngest princess, and she cried out to her sisters, "Something is wrong; someone took hold of my gown."

"You silly girl!" said the eldest, "it is nothing but a nail in the wall."

Down they all went, and at the bottom they found themselves in a most delightful grove of trees; and the leaves were all of silver, and glittered and sparkled beautifully. The soldier wished to take away some token of the place, so he broke off a little branch, and there came a loud noise from the tree. Then the youngest daughter said again, "I am sure all is not right—didn't you hear that noise? That never happened before."

But the eldest said, "It is only our princes, who are shouting for joy at our approach."

They came to another grove of trees, where all the leaves were of gold; and afterwards to a third, where the leaves were all glittering diamonds. And the soldier broke a branch from each; and every time there was a loud noise, which made the youngest sister tremble with fear. But the eldest still said it was only the princes, who were crying for joy.

They went on until they came to a great lake, and at the side of the lake there lay twelve little boats with twelve handsome princes in them, who seemed to be waiting there for the princesses.

One of the princesses went into each boat, and the soldier stepped into the same boat as the youngest. As they were rowing over the lake, the prince who was in the boat with the youngest princess and the soldier said, "I do not know why it is, but though I am rowing with all my might we are moving much more slowly than usual, and I am quite tired—the boat seems very heavy today."

"It is only the heat of the weather," said the princess, "I am very warm, too."

On the other side of the lake stood a fine, illuminated castle from which came the merry music of horns and trumpets. There they all landed, and went into the castle, and each prince danced with his princess; and the soldier, who was still invisible, danced with them too. When any of the princesses had a cup of wine set by her, he drank it all up, so that when she put the cup to her mouth it was empty. At this, too, the youngest sister was terribly frightened, but the eldest always silenced her.

They danced on till three o'clock in the morning, and then all their shoes were worn out, so that they were obliged to leave. The princes rowed them back again over the lake (but this time the soldier placed himself in the boat with the eldest princess); and on the opposite shore they took leave of each other, the princesses promising to come again the next night.

When they came to the stairs, the soldier ran on before the princesses, and laid himself down. And as the twelve, tired sisters slowly came up, they heard him snoring in his bed and they said, "Now all is quite safe." Then they undressed themselves, put away their fine clothes, pulled off their shoes, and went to bed.

In the morning the soldier said nothing about what had happened, but was determined to see more of this strange adventure, and went again on the second and third nights. Everything happened just as before: the princesses danced till their shoes were worn to pieces, and then returned home. On the third night the soldier carried away one of the golden cups as a token of where he had been.

As soon as the time came when he was to declare the secret, he was taken before the king with the three branches and the golden cup, and the twelve princesses stood listening behind the door to hear what he would say.

The king asked him. "Where do my twelve daughters dance at night?"

The soldier answered, "With twelve princes in a castle underground." And then he told the king all that had happened, and showed him the three branches and the golden cup, which he had brought with him.

The king called for the princesses, and asked them whether what the soldier said was true and when they saw that they were discovered, and that it was of no use to deny what had happened, they confessed it all.

So the king asked the soldier which of the princesses he would ask to be his wife; and he answered, "I am not very young, so I will ask the eldest." And the eldest agreed to marry him, as long as her sisters could continue to visit the underground castle, and that she and the prince could visit together on occassion, too. The prince agreed happily and they were married that very day, and the soldier was chosen to be the king's heir.

Little Jack Horner,
Sat in the corner,
Eating a Christmas pie;
He put in his thumb,
And he took out a plum,
And said,
"What a good boy am I!"

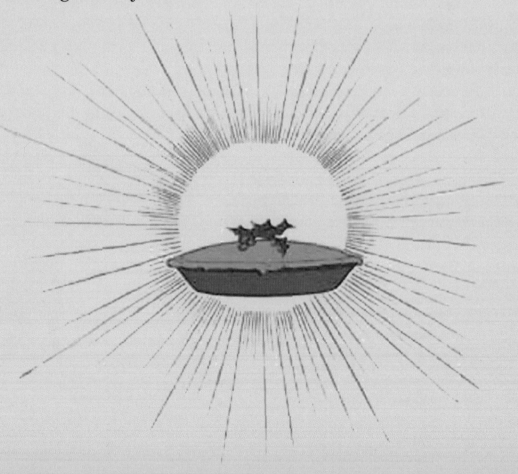

Humpty-Dumpty sat on a wall,
Humpty-Dumpty had a great fall;
All the king's horses, and all the king's men
Cannot put Humpty-Dumpty
Together again.

"If history were taught in the form of stories, it would never be forgotten."

~Rudyard Kipling

Rapunzel

There once lived a man and his wife, who had long wished for a child, but in vain. Now there was at the back of their house a little window which over-looked a beautiful garden full of the finest vegetables and flowers; but there was a high wall all round it, and no one ventured into it, for it belonged to a witch of great might, and of whom all the world was afraid. One day while the wife was standing at the window and looking into the garden, she saw a garden bed filled with the finest rampion*; and it looked so fresh and green that she began to wish for some; and at length she longed for it greatly. This went on for days, and as she knew she could not get the rampion, she pined away, and grew pale and miserable. Then the man was uneasy, and asked, "What is the matter, dear wife?" "Oh," answered she, "I shall die unless I can have some of that rampion to eat that grows in the garden at the back of our house." The man, who loved her very much, thought to himself, "Rather than lose my wife I will get some rampion, cost what it will."

So, in the twilight, he climbed over the wall into the witch's garden, plucked hastily a handful of rampion, and brought it to his wife. She made a salad of it at once, and ate of it to her heart's content. But she liked it so much, and it tasted so good, that the next day she longed for it even more than she had before; if she was to have any rest the man must climb over the wall once more. So he went in the twilight again, and as he was climbing back, he saw, all at once, the witch standing before him, and was terribly frightened, as she cried, with angry eyes,

---

* Rampion is an edible root that is delicious in salads.

"How dare you climb over into my garden like a thief, and steal my rampion!" "Oh," answered he, " be merciful rather than just, I have only done it through necessity; for my wife saw your rampion out of the window, and was so desperate for it that she would have died if she could not have had some to eat."

Then the witch said, "If it is all as you say, you may have as much rampion as you like, on one condition: you must give your first child to me. The child will have a good life with me, and I will care for it like a mother." In his distress of mind the man promised everything, and when the child was born, the witch appeared, and, giving the child the name of Rapunzel (which is the same as rampion), she took it away with her.

Rapunzel was the most beautiful child in the world. When she was twelve years old the witch shut her up in a tower in the woods. The tower didn't have steps or a door, only a small window above. When the witch wished to be let in, she would stand below and would cry, "Rapunzel, Rapunzel! let down your hair." Rapunzel had beautiful long hair that shone like gold. When she heard the voice of the witch she would undo the fastening of the upper window, let loose her long braided hair, and let it down until it reached the ground below, and the witch would climb up by it. After they had lived thus a few years it happened that as the king's son was riding through the wood, he came to the tower, and as he drew near he heard a voice singing so sweetly that he stood still and listened. It was Rapunzel in her loneliness trying to pass away the time with sweet songs. The king's son wished to go in to her, and tried to find a door in the tower, but there was none. So he rode home, but the song had entered into his heart, and every day he went into the wood and listened to it.

Once, as he was standing there under a tree, he saw the witch come up, and listened while she called out, "O Rapunzel, Rapunzel! Let down your hair." Then he saw how Rapunzel let down her long hair, and how the witch climbed up by it and went in to her, and he said to himself, "Since that is the ladder, I will climb it and see who sings such a lovely song."

The next day, as soon as it began to grow dusk, he went to the tower and cried, "O Rapunzel, Rapunzel! Let down your hair." And she let down her hair, and the king's son climbed up by it. Rapunzel was greatly terrified when she saw that a man had come in to her room, for she had never seen one before; but the king's son began speaking so kindly to her, and told how her singing had entered into his heart, so that he could have no peace until he had seen her. Then Rapunzel forgot her terror, and when he asked her to take him for her husband, and she saw that he was young and handsome, she thought to herself, "I certainly like him much better than old mother Gothel," and she put her hand into his hand, saying, "I would willingly go with thee, but I do not know how I shall get out. When thou comest, bring each time a silken rope, and I will make a ladder, and when it is quite ready I will get down by it out of the tower, and thou shalt take me away on thy horse."

They agreed that he should come to her every evening, as the old woman came in the daytime. So the witch knew nothing of all this until once Rapunzel said to her unwittingly, "Mother Gothel, how is it that you climb up here so slowly, and the king's son is with me in a moment?" "O wicked child," cried the witch, "what is this I hear? I thought I had hidden thee from all the world, and thou hast betrayed me!" In her anger she seized Rapunzel, picked up a pair of scissors, and roughly began to chop off all of Rapunzel's beautiful hair. Then she took Rapunzel out to a distant desert and left her there all alone.

The same day on which she took Rapunzel away, she went back to the tower in the evening and wove together the cut hair and secured it to the window. The king's son came and cried, "Rapunzel, Rapunzel! Let down your hair." Then she let the hair down, and the king's son climbed up, but instead of his dearest Rapunzel, he found the witch looking at him with wicked glittering eyes. "Aha!" cried she, mocking him, "you came for your darling, but the sweet bird sits no longer in the nest, and sings no more! Rapunzel is lost to you, you will see her no more."

The king's son was beside himself with grief, and in his agony he jumped from the tower: he escaped with his life, but the thorns on which he fell caused him to become blind. He wandered blind through the wood, eating nothing but roots and berries, and doing nothing but lament and weep for the loss of his dear Rapunzel. After a long while, he neared the desert place where Rapunzel lived and heard a sweet, familiar voice singing in the distance. He went toward it and, when he realized it was Rapunzel's own sweet voice, he ran to her and fell into her arms. She began to weep with joy as well and when her tears touched his eyes they became clear again, and he could see with them as well as ever. Then he took her to his kingdom, where he was received with great joy, and there they lived long and happily.

"Some stories are true that never happened."

~Elie Wiesel

Mary had a little lamb, Its fleece was white as snow;
And everywhere that Mary went, The lamb was sure to go.

He followed her to school one day;
That was against the rule;
It made the children laugh and play
To see a lamb at school.

Sleeping Beauty

Adapted from the Grimm Brothers' tale

*L*ong ago there lived a king and queen who longed for a child but could not have one.

One day, while the queen was swimming in the river behind the palace, a frog came out of the water and squatted on the ground near her. He said to the queen, "Thy wish shall be fulfilled; before a year has gone by, thou shall bring a daughter into the world."

And as the frog foretold, so it happened, and the queen bore a daughter whom they named Rosamond. She was so beautiful that the king was overjoyed and planned a great feast. He invited all his relatives, all his friends, and everyone he knew. At the last minute, he decided he should also invite the wise women of the kingdom so that they would be kind to the child. There were thirteen of them in his kingdom, but he only had twelve golden plates for them to eat from and there was no time left to find a thirteenth, so he didn't invite the youngest one of the thirteen wise women.

The feast was celebrated with great splendor. As it drew to an end, the wise women stood in line to present to the child their wonderful gifts. One bestowed virtue, one beauty, a third riches, and so on. When eleven of them had offered their gifts, the uninvited thirteenth appeared, angry and anxious for revenge.

She cried with a loud voice, "In her fifteenth year, the princess shall prick herself with a spindle and shall fall down dead."

Shocked and scared, all the guests left the feast quickly without saying a word to each other.

The next day, the twelfth wise woman came to the castle to see the king and queen because she had not had a chance to bestow her gift at the feast. She told them that though she could not do away with the evil prophecy, she could at least soften it. So she said,

"The princess shall not die, but shall fall into a deep sleep for a hundred years."

Now the king, anxious to save his child from death or even a hundred years of sleep, made a new law that all the spindles in his kingdom should be burnt up. The princess grew up, adorned with all the gifts of the wise women so that she was so lovely, modest, sweet, kind, and clever, that no one who saw her could help loving her.

One day, when Rosamond was fifteen years old, the king and queen had to take a trip to another kingdom, and the princess was left alone in the castle. It was the first time she was home alone and she spent the whole afternoon exploring. She wandered about into all the nooks and corners, and into all the chambers and parlours, until at last she came to an old tower. She climbed the narrow winding stair which led to a little door with a rusty key sticking out of the lock. She turned the key and the door opened, and there in the little room sat an old woman with a spindle, diligently spinning her flax.

"Good day, mother," said Rosamond, "what are you doing?"

"I am spinning," answered the old woman, nodding her head.

"What is that thing that twists around so quickly?" asked the princess, taking the spindle into her hand and beginning to spin it around. No sooner had she touched it than the evil prophecy was fulfilled, and she pricked her finger with it. In that very moment she fell back upon the bed that stood there, and lay in a deep sleep. And this sleep fell upon the whole castle so that the king and queen, who had returned and were in the great hall, fell fast asleep, and with them the whole court. The horses in their stalls, the dogs in the yard, the pigeons on the roof, the flies on the wall, the very fire that flickered on the hearth, became still, and slept like the rest. The meat on the spit ceased roasting, and the cook, who was stirring together a pudding, lay down by the fire and fell fast asleep. The wind ceased, and not a leaf fell from the trees about the castle.

Around the castle there grew a hedge of thorns that became thicker every year, until at last the whole castle was hidden from view, and nothing of it could be seen but the weathervane on the roof. Rumors of the sleeping castle and the beautiful sleeping princess spread through the country, and from time to time many princes came and tried to force their way through the hedge to see if the story was true, but none could get through.

Many years later a prince came through the land and overheard an old man telling someone about a castle standing behind the hedge of thorns, and that there was a beautiful enchanted princess named Rosamond within who had slept for a hundred years, and with her the king and queen, and the whole court. The old man had been told by his grandfather that many king's sons had tried to pass the thorn-hedge, but had been caught and pierced by the thorns, and many had died there. Then said the young prince, "I am not afraid to try. I shall fight my way through the thorny hedge and see the lovely Rosamond." The good old man tried to dissuade him, but the prince would not listen to his words. It had now been a hundred years since the castle had fallen asleep.

When the prince drew near the hedge of thorns, it was transformed into a hedge of beautiful large flowers, which parted and bent aside to let him pass, and then closed behind him in a thick hedge. When he reached the castle-yard, he saw the horses and dogs lying asleep, and on the roof the pigeons were sitting with their heads under their wings. And when he came indoors, the flies on the wall were asleep and the cook in the kitchen was lying on the hearth. He began to climb the stairs and saw in the hall the whole court lying asleep, and above them, on their thrones, slept the king and the queen. He kept climbing through the eerie silence—it was so quiet that he could hear his own breathing. At last he came to the tower, went up the winding stairway, and opened the door of the little room where Rosamond lay. When he saw her looking so lovely in her sleep, he could not turn away his eyes. He stooped and kissed her, and immediately she opened her eyes and looked up at him very kindly. After a few moments she asked about her mother and father. The prince led her downstairs, where the king and the queen and the whole court were awake and looking around in great wonder. The horses in the yard got up and shook themselves, the hounds sprang up and wagged their tails, the pigeons on the roof drew their heads from under their wings, looked round, and flew into the field, the flies on the wall crept on a little farther, the kitchen fire leapt up and blazed and cooked the meat, the joint on the spit began to roast, and the cook stood up and brushed off her apron.

The prince explained to Rosamond and the king and queen how he had found them and as he was speaking, the princess began to fall in love. It was not long before Rosamond and the prince were married at the castle. The whole kingdom came to the feast to meet the princess who had slept for a hundred years and to wish the couple great happiness. This time the king was sure to invite all the wise women of the land, and Rosamond and the prince were blessed with great joy, love, and peace for the rest of their lives.

"Today a reader, tomorrow a leader."

~Margaret Fuller

Hey! Diddle, diddle,
The cat and the fiddle,
The cow jumped over the moon;
The little dog laughed
To see such sport,
And the dish ran away with the spoon.

The Tale of Peter Rabbit

By Beatrix Potter

Once upon a time there were four little Rabbits, and their names were Flopsy, Mopsy, Cotton-tail, and Peter.

They lived with their Mother in a sand-bank, underneath the root of a very big fir-tree.

"Now my dears," said old Mrs. Rabbit one morning, "you may go into the fields or down the lane, but don't go into Mr. McGregor's garden: your father had an accident there; he was put in a pie by Mrs. McGregor."

"Now run along, and don't get into mischief. I am going out."

Then old Mrs. Rabbit took a basket and her umbrella, and went through the wood to the baker's. She bought a loaf of brown bread and five currant buns.

Flopsy, Mopsy, and Cotton-tail, who were good little bunnies, went down the lane to gather blackberries.

But Peter, who was very naughty, ran straight away to Mr. McGregor's garden, and squeezed under the gate!

First he ate some lettuces and some French beans; and then he ate some radishes;

And then, feeling rather sick, he went to look for some parsley.

But round the end of a cucumber frame, whom should he meet but Mr. McGregor!

Mr. McGregor was on his hands and knees planting out young cabbages, but he jumped up and ran after Peter, waving a rake and calling out,

"Stop thief!"

Peter was most dreadfully frightened; he rushed all over the garden, for he had forgotten the way back to the gate.

He lost one of his shoes among the cabbages, and the other shoe amongst the potatoes.

After losing them, he ran on four legs and went faster, so that I think he might have got away altogether if he had not unfortunately run into a gooseberry net, and got caught by the large buttons on his jacket. It was a blue jacket with brass buttons, quite new.

Peter gave himself up for lost, and shed big tears; but his sobs were overheard by some friendly sparrows, who flew to him in great excitement, and implored him to exert himself.

Mr. McGregor came up with a sieve, which he intended to pop upon the top of Peter; but Peter wriggled out just in time, leaving his jacket behind him.

He rushed into the tool-shed, and jumped into a can. It would have been a beautiful thing to hide in, if it had not had so much water in it.

Mr. McGregor was quite sure that Peter was somewhere in the tool-shed, perhaps hidden underneath a flower-pot. He began to turn them over carefully, looking under each.

Presently Peter sneezed—"Kertyschoo!" Mr. McGregor was after him in no time.

He tried to put his foot upon Peter, who jumped out of a window, upsetting three plants. The window was too small for Mr. McGregor, and he was tired of running after Peter. He went back to his work.

Peter sat down to rest; he was out of breath and trembling with fright, and he had not the least idea which way to go. Also he was very damp with sitting in that can.

After a time he began to wander about, going lippity—lippity—not very fast, and looking all round.

He found a door in a wall but it was locked, and there was no room for a fat little rabbit to squeeze underneath.

An old mouse was running in and out over the stone doorstep, carrying peas and beans to her family in the wood. Peter asked her the way to the gate, but she had such a large pea in her mouth that she could not answer. She only shook her head at him. Peter began to cry.

Then he tried to find his way straight across the garden, but he became more and more puzzled. Presently, he came to a pond where Mr. McGregor filled his water-cans. A white cat was staring at some gold-fish; she sat very, very still, but now and then the tip of her tail twitched as if it were alive. Peter thought it best to go away without speaking to her; he had heard about cats from his cousin, little Benjamin Bunny.

He went back towards the tool-shed, but suddenly, quite close to him, he heard the noise of a hoe—*scr-r-ritch, scratch, scratch, scritch*. Peter scuttered underneath the bushes. But presently, as nothing happened, he came out, and climbed upon a wheelbarrow and peeped over.

The first thing he saw was Mr. McGregor hoeing onions. His back was turned towards Peter, and beyond him was the gate!

Peter got down very quietly off the wheelbarrow; and started running as fast as he could go, along a straight walk behind some black-currant bushes.

Mr. McGregor caught sight of him at the corner, but Peter did not care. He slipped underneath the gate, and was safe at last in the wood outside the garden.

Mr. McGregor hung up the little jacket and the shoes for a scare-crow to frighten the blackbirds.

Peter never stopped running or looked behind him till he got home to the big fir-tree.

He was so tired that he flopped down upon the nice soft sand on the floor of the rabbit-hole and shut his eyes. His mother was busy cooking; she wondered what he had done with his clothes. It was the second little jacket and pair of shoes that Peter had lost in a fortnight!

I am sorry to say that Peter was not very well during the evening.

His mother put him to bed, and made some chamomile tea; and she gave a dose of it to Peter!

"One tablespoonful to be taken at bed-time."

But Flopsy, Mopsy, and Cotton-tail had bread and milk and blackberries for supper.

THE END

The Three Bears

$\mathcal{L}$ ittle Goldilocks was a pretty girl who lived once upon a time in a far-off country.

One day she was sitting on the hearth in front of the fireplace playing with her two kittens. After a while, she began to get antsy and decided to take a walk.

She got up and trotted away into the woods behind her mother's house, and it was such a warm, pleasant day that she wandered on and on until she came into a part of the woods where she had never been before.

Now, in this wood there lived a family of three bears. The first was a GREAT BIG BEAR, the second was a MIDDLE-SIZED BEAR, and the third was a LITTLE TEENY TINY BEAR, and they all lived together in a funny little house where they were very happy.

Goldilocks stopped when she came to the bears' house, and began to wonder who lived there.

"I'll just look in and see," she said, and so she did; but there was no one there, for the bears had all gone out for a morning walk while the soup they were going to have for dinner cooled on the table.

Goldilocks was rather hungry after her walk, and the soup smelled so good that she began to wish the people of the house would come home and invite her to have some. But although she looked everywhere, under the table and into the cupboards, she couldn't find anyone, and at last she could resist no longer. She decided to take just a little sip to see how the soup tasted. The soup had been put into three bowls—a Great Big Bowl for the Great Big Bear, a Middle-sized

Bowl for the Middle-sized Bear, and a Teeny Tiny Bowl for the Teeny Tiny Bear. Beside each bowl lay a spoon, and Goldilocks took one and helped herself to a spoonful of soup from the Great Big Bowl.

Ugh! How it burnt her mouth! It was so hot and peppery that she did not like it at all. Still, she was very hungry, so she thought she would try again.

This time she took a sip of the Middle-sized Bear's soup, but she didn't like it any better, for it was too salty. But when she tasted the Teeny Tiny Bear's soup it was just as she liked it; so she ate it up, every drop, without thinking twice about it.

When she had finished her dinner she noticed three chairs standing by the wall. One was a Great Big Chair, which she climbed up on and sat down. Oh, dear! How hard it was! She was sure she could not sit there for long, so she climbed up on the next, which was only a Middle-sized Chair, but that was too soft for her taste, so she went on to the last, which was a Teeny Tiny Chair and suited her exactly.

It was so comfortable that she sat on and on until, if you'll believe it, the bottom fell out! Then, of course, she was comfortable no longer, so she got up and began to wonder what she should do next.

There was a staircase in the bears' house, and Goldilocks thought she would go up it and see where it led to. So up she went, and when she reached the top she laughed out loud, for the bears' bedroom was the funniest she had ever seen. In the middle of the room stood a Great Big Bed, on one side of it there was a Middle-sized Bed, and on the other side there was a Teeny Tiny Bed.

Goldilocks was sleepy, so she thought she would lie down and have a little nap. First she got up on the Great Big Bed, but it was just as hard as the Great Big Chair had been, so she jumped off and tried the Middle-sized Bed, but it was so soft that she sank right down into the feather cushions and was nearly smothered.

"I will try the Teeny Tiny Bed," she said, and so she did, and it was so comfortable that she soon fell fast asleep.

While she lay there, dreaming of all sorts of pleasant things, the three bears came home from their walk very hungry and quite ready for their dinners.

But, oh! Dear me! How cross the Great Big Bear looked when he saw his spoon had been used and thrown under the table.

"WHO HAS BEEN TASTING MY SOUP?" he cried, in a Great Big Voice.

"AND WHO HAS BEEN TASTING MINE?" cried the Middle-sized Bear, in a Middle-sized Voice.

"BUT WHO HAS BEEN TASTING MINE AND TASTED IT ALL UP?" cried the poor little Teeny Tiny Bear in a Teeny Tiny Voice, with the tears running down his Teeny Tiny Face.

When the Great Big Bear went to sit down in his Great Big Chair, he cried out in his Great Big Voice:
"WHO HAS BEEN SITTING ON MY CHAIR?"

And the Middle-sized Bear cried, in a Middle-sized Voice:
"WHO HAS BEEN SITTING ON MY CHAIR?"

But the Teeny Tiny Bear cried out in a Teeny Tiny Voice of anger:
"WHO HAS BEEN SITTING ON MY CHAIR, AND SAT THE BOTTOM OUT?"

By this time the bears were sure that someone had been in their house quite recently, so they looked about to see if someone were still there.

There was certainly no one downstairs, so they went up the staircase to their bedroom.

As soon as the Great Big Bear looked at his bed, he cried out, in his Great Big Voice:
"WHO HAS BEEN LYING ON MY BED?"

And the Middle-sized Bear, seeing that the coverlet was all rumpled, cried out, in a Middle-sized Voice:
"WHO HAS BEEN LYING ON MY BED?"

But the Teeny Tiny Bear cried out, in a Teeny Tiny Voice of astonishment: "WHO HAS BEEN LYING ON MY BED AND LIES THERE STILL?"

Now, when the Great Big Bear began to speak, Goldilocks dreamt that there was a bee buzzing in the room, and when the Middle-sized Bear began to speak, she dreamt that it was flying out of the window; but when the Teeny Tiny Bear began to speak, she dreamt that the bee had come back and stung her on the ear, and up she jumped. Oh! How frightened she was when she saw the three bears standing beside her.

She hopped out of bed and in a second was out through the open window. Never stopping to wonder if the fall had hurt her, she got up and ran and ran and ran until she could go no farther, always thinking that the bears were close behind her. And when at length she fell down in a heap on the ground, because she was too tired to run any more, it was her own mother who picked her up, because in her fright she had run straight home without knowing it.

Hickery, dickery, dock,
The mouse ran up the clock;
The clock struck one,
Down the mouse ran,
Hickery, dickery, dock.

Mary, Mary, quite contrary,
How does your garden grow?
With silver bells, and cockle shells,
And cowslips all of a row.

"Grandmas never run out of hugs or cookies."

~Author Unknown

Records

"When you look at your life, the greatest happinesses are family happinesses."

~Joyce Brothers

"You don't choose your family. They are God's gift to you, as you are to them."

~Desmond Tutu

Family Tree

SHARING family history can be one of the most meaningful aspects of grand-parenting. On the following pages is a simple family tree for you to fill out with your grandchild or grandchildren. As you write in the family names, take time to share any special stories you know about each person. It's the stories that will stick in the little ones' minds, connecting them to their roots for years to come.

Write your name in the "Grandma" box and then fill in the generations above and below you. Below is an example.

Lilly Jones   Jonathon Jones   GRANDCHILDREN   Andrew Dwyer   GRANDCHILDREN

Jennifer D. Jones   CHILDREN   Peter Dwyer   Laura Dwyer   CHILDREN

John Dwyer   GRANDPA   Lillian Dwyer   GRANDMA

James Dwyer   GREAT GRANDPA   Anna L. Dwyer   GREAT GRANDMA   Peter Smith   GREAT GRANDPA   Abigail M. Smith   GREAT GRANDMA

GRANDCHILDREN

CHILDREN

GRANDMA

GREAT GRANDPA   GREAT GRANDMA

"In different hours, a man represents each of several of his ancestors, as if there were seven or eight of us rolled up in each man's skin,—seven or eight ancestors at least, and they constitute the variety of notes for that new piece of music which his life is."

~Ralph Waldo Emerson

Family Treasure Map

ON the next couple of pages is a treasure map where you can mark the places where your ancestors came from, sharing any stories you know with your grandchildren as you locate the spots on the map together. Don't be afraid to write on the pages. Use this as a tool to start sharing family history with your grandchildren. Below is an example.

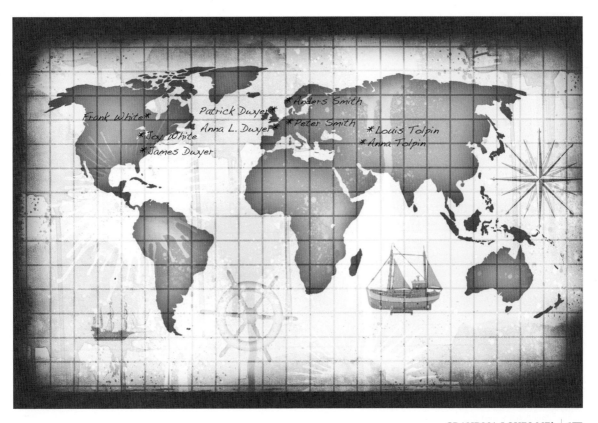

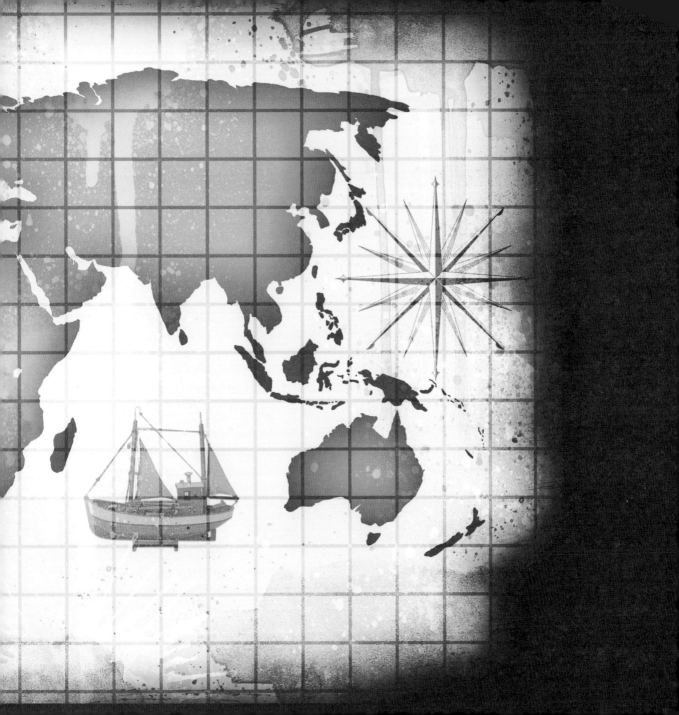

Important Dates

USE these pages to record birthdays, anniversaries, and other important dates in your family's lives.

JANUARY

1	
2	
3	
4	
5	
6	
7	
8	
9	
10	
11	
12	
13	

14

15

16

17

18

19

20

21

22

23

24

25

26

27

28

29

30

31

FEBRUARY

1

2

3

4

5

6

7

8

9

10

11

12

13

14

15

16

17

18

19

20

21

22

23

24

25

26

27

28

29

MARCH

1
2
3
4
5
6
7
8
9
10
11
12
13
14
15

16

17

18

19

20

21

22

23

24

25

26

27

28

29

30

31

APRIL

1

2

3

4

5

6

7

8

9

10

11

12

13

14

15

16

17

18

19

20

21

22

23

24

25

26

27

28

29

30

MAY

1

2

3

4

5

6

7

8

9

10

11

12

13

14

15

16 _____

17 _____

18 _____

19 _____

20 _____

21 _____

22 _____

23 _____

24 _____

25 _____

26 _____

27 _____

28 _____

29 _____

30 _____

31 _____

JUNE

1

2

3

4

5

6

7

8

9

10

11

12

13

14

15

16 _____

17 _____

18 _____

19 _____

20 _____

21 _____

22 _____

23 _____

24 _____

25 _____

26 _____

27 _____

28 _____

29 _____

30 _____

_____

JULY

1

2

3

4

5

6

7

8

9

10

11

12

13

14

15

16

17

18

19

20

21

22

23

24

25

26

27

28

29

30

31

AUGUST

1

2

3

4

5

6

7

8

9

10

11

12

13

14

15

16

17

18

19

20

21

22

23

24

25

26

27

28

29

30

31

SEPTEMBER

1

2

3

4

5

6

7

8

9

10

11

12

13

14

15

16

17

18

19

20

21

22

23

24

25

26

27

28

29

30

OCTOBER

1

2

3

4

5

6

7

8

9

10

11

12

13

14

15

16 _____

17 _____

18 _____

19 _____

20 _____

21 _____

22 _____

23 _____

24 _____

25 _____

26 _____

27 _____

28 _____

29 _____

30 _____

31 _____

NOVEMBER

1

2

3

4

5

6

7

8

9

10

11

12

13

14

15

16

17

18

19

20

21

22

23

24

25

26

27

28

29

30

DECEMBER

1

2

3

4

5

6

7

8

9

10

11

12

13

14

15

16 _____

17 _____

18 _____

19 _____

20 _____

21 _____

22 _____

23 _____

24 _____

25 _____

26 _____

27 _____

28 _____

29 _____

30 _____

31 _____

Important Facts

USE these pages to record important information about your grandchildren and their parents.

EMERGENCY INFORMATION

Parents' contact information

Home:

_____

_____

_____

_____

_____

Work:

_____

_____

_____

_____

_____

Pediatrician contact:

_____
_____
_____
_____
_____

Allergies:

Foods:

_____
_____
_____
_____
_____
_____

Medicines:

_____
_____
_____
_____
_____
_____

School name and address:

_____

_____

_____

_____

_____

Classroom number:

_____

_____

_____

_____

_____

Teachers:

_____

_____

_____

_____

_____

OTHER USEFUL INFORMATION

Favorite foods:

_____

_____

_____

Favorite colors:

_____

_____

_____

_____

_____

_____

Favorite activities:

_____

_____

_____

_____

_____

_____

Clothing sizes:

_____

_____

_____

_____

_____

_____

_____

_____

_____

A Grandma's Journal

"The happiest moments of my life have been the few which I have passed at home in the bosom of my family."

~Thomas Jefferson

Conversation Time

THERE may not be any activity more important than simply talking with your grandchildren. Make some hot chocolate, cozy up on the sofa, and take turns responding to the prompts below. Record your answers as a keepsake of your time together. Someday your grandchild will be thrilled to find these pages and remember the time you spent really getting to know each other.

Grandma: My very earliest memory is . . .

_____

_____

_____

_____

Child: My very earliest memory is . . .

_____

_____

_____

_____

Grandma: When I was your age, my favorite things to do were . . .

_____

_____

_____

_____

Child: My favorite things to do are . . .

_____

_____

_____

_____

Grandma: My favorite toys were . . .

_____

_____

_____

_____

Child: My favorite toys are . . .

_____

_____

_____

_____

Grandma: My favorite teacher was . . .

_____

_____

_____

_____

Child: My favorite teacher is . . .

_____

_____

_____

_____

Grandma: When I was young, I was afraid of . . .

_____

_____

_____

_____

Child: Sometimes I'm afraid of . . .

_____

_____

_____

_____

Grandma: My favorite food is . . .

_____

_____

_____

_____

Child: My favorite food is . . .

_____

_____

_____

_____

Grandma: My favorite thing to do with my grandchild[ren] is . . .

_____
_____
_____
_____

Child: My favorite thing to do with my grandparent[s] is . . .

_____
_____
_____
_____

Grandma: My favorite book is . . .

_____
_____
_____
_____

Child: My favorite book is . . .

_____
_____
_____
_____

Grandma: If I could have three wishes, they would be . . .

_____
_____
_____
_____

Child: If I could have three wishes, they would be . . .

_____
_____
_____
_____

Grandma: The most fun I ever had was when . . .

_____
_____
_____
_____

Child: The most fun I ever had was when . . .

_____
_____
_____
_____

Grandma: One thing I do NOT like to do is . . .

_____
_____
_____
_____

Child: One thing I do NOT like to do is . . .

_____
_____
_____
_____

Grandma: The farthest away from home I've ever been is . . .

_____

_____

_____

_____

Child: The farthest away from home I've ever been is . . .

_____

_____

_____

_____

Grandma: The hardest thing about being my age is . . .

_____

_____

_____

_____

Child: The hardest thing about being my age is . . .

_____

_____

_____

_____

Grandma: The best thing about being my age is . . .

_____

_____

_____

_____

Child: The best thing about being my age is . . .

_____

_____

_____

_____

Grandma: Someday I would like to . . .

_____

_____

_____

_____

Child: Someday I would like to . . .

_____

_____

_____

_____

Grandma: Here's a funny story about your mother or father . . .

_____

_____

_____

_____

Child: Here's a funny story about my mother or father . . .

_____

_____

_____

_____

Grandma: The most amazing thing about me is . . .

_____

_____

_____

_____

Child: The most amazing thing about me is . . .

_____

_____

_____

_____

Grandma: If I could change three things about myself, they would be . . .

_____

_____

_____

_____

Child: If I could change three things about myself, they would be . . .

_____

_____

_____

_____

Grandma: Something most people don't know about me is . . .

_____

_____

_____

_____

Child: Something most people don't know about me is . . .

_____

_____

_____

_____

Grandma: The nicest thing someone has ever done for me is . . .

_____

_____

_____

_____

Child: The nicest thing someone has ever done for me is . . .

_____

_____

_____

_____

Grandma: If I could be invisible for one whole day, I would . . .

_____

_____

_____

_____

Child: If I could be invisible for one whole day, I would . . .

_____

_____

_____

_____

Grandma: One of the hardest things I ever did was . . .

_____

_____

_____

_____

Child: One of the hardest things I ever did was . . .

_____

_____

_____

_____

Grandma: If I had to describe God using only three words, they'd be . . .

_____

_____

_____

_____

Child: If I had to describe God using only three words, they'd be . . .

_____

_____

_____

_____

Grandma: Growing up, the best thing about my house was . . .

_____

_____

_____

_____

Child: The best thing about my house is . . .

_____

_____

_____

_____

Grandma: One thing I'm not very good at is . . .

_____

_____

_____

_____

Child: One thing I'm not very good at is . . .

_____

_____

_____

_____

Grandma: One thing I'm really good at is . . .

_____

_____

_____

_____

Child: One thing I'm really good at is . . .

_____

_____

_____

_____

Grandma: One thing I hope you'll always remember is . . .

_____
_____
_____
_____

Child: One thing I hope you'll always remember is . . .

_____
_____
_____
_____

Favorite Quotes from the Grandkids

IT'S so easy to forget the wonderful things kids say almost as soon as you've heard them. Use these pages to write them down so you'll have them to remember for years to come.

_____

_____

_____

_____

_____

_____

_____

_____

_____

_____

_____

_____

Acknowledgments and Art Credits

This book was a pleasure to put together, thanks largely to those who participated.

Mom, thank you for contributing your wonderful illustrations! I've always wanted to do a book together. Thanks for investing so much into this project on such short notice.

Much of the art in this book that was not done by Martha M. Gehring originated from artists of the nineteenth and early twentieth century and has been retouched to enhance the quality. The artists represented are:

Anne Anderson: page 22
Arthur Rackham: pages 36 and 57
Beatrix Potter: pages 153–157, 60, 72, and 94
Bessie Collins Pease: pages 19 and 25
Edmund DuLac: page 106
Eleanor Vere Boyle: page 11
Frederick Richardson: pages 158–165
George Cruikshank: pages 100 and 103
Jessie Wilcox Smith: pages 16, 31, 149, 63, 89, 208, and 221

John Maler Collier: page 144
Kate Greenaway: pages 9, 55, 75, 86, 90, 104–105, 109, 168, and 227
Kay Nielsen: pages 126 and 131
National Association of Autobon Societies, Bird Lore, 1899: page 6
Richard Doyle: page 7
Ruth Mary Hallock: page 48
Vilhelm Pedersen: page 112
W. W. Denslow: pages 98–99, 110–111, 124–125, 132–133, 134,
142–143, 150–151, 166–167